Praise for *Son of Elsewhere*

"*Son of Elsewhere* is a memoir that is immense in its desire to give, and not just of its writer's life and history. But it is also a rich offering of image, of music, of place. I am thankful for the touchable nature of this story, the movements within the book, and how visual this journey is."

—Hanif Abdurraqib, author of *A Little Devil in America: In Praise of Black Performance*

"It is astounding how accurately and honestly Elamin Abdelmahmoud manages to map the strange territory between cultures that so many migrants call home. The interlinked essays in this collection, which filter the immigrant experience through everything from country music to professional-wrestling fan fiction, manage to pull off a rare trick—at once sincere, ironic, hilarious, and profound. *Son of Elsewhere* is the sort of book that can only come from a writer both incisive and open-hearted. Abdelmahmoud, to our great fortune, is both."

—Omar El Akkad, Scotiabank Giller Prize–winning author of *What Strange Paradise* and *American War*

"*Son of Elsewhere* is a profound, tender collection of stories that speaks to those who exist in and out of liminal spaces. It's a narrative that forces readers to interrogate Blackness beyond American borders, American exceptionalism at the expense of Black and Brown people, and identity between separate languages. Elamin Abdelmahmoud is a skillful cartographer of place, architecture, and human emotion, blending them together so effortlessly that one will walk away from this debut seeing the symphony—and collision—in the mundane and the extraordinary. With this book, Abdelmahmoud announces that he is here, and we should be so thankful for that."

—Morgan Jerkins, *New York Times* bestselling author of *This Will Be My Undoing, Wandering in Strange Lands,* and *Caul Baby*

"*Son of Elsewhere* is marvelous and wise and fascinating. An introspective rumination on identity, belonging, and otherness that is breezily told but deeply felt. Like a conversation with one of your smartest friends, Elamin Abdelmahmoud's book offers a unique perspective that feels both familiar and challenging. It's a privilege to read."

—R. Eric Thomas, national bestselling author of *Here for It: Or, How to Save Your Soul in America*

"Elamin Abdelmahmoud's *Son of Elsewhere* achieves what all nonfiction work should: a unique type of universality. His writing feels like a magic trick—every page is charming, funny, and yet painful—a collection that presses on your most tender feelings, like a bruise yet to heal. *Son of Elsewhere* is a salve."

—Scaachi Koul, author of *One Day We'll All Be Dead and None of This Will Matter*

"Elamin Abdelmahmoud is full of light and wisdom; his book is no different. With humor and vulnerability, he writes about the struggle to find himself in Canada while maintaining a connection to his roots in Sudan. I laughed out loud even as my heart ached for him, and I dog-eared dozens of pages where his sentences were so perfect that I will return to them again and again. *Son of Elsewhere* is witty and tender and the story of a lovely writer discovering himself, a person I am so glad to call a friend."

—Rosemary Barton, host of CBC's
Rosemary Barton Live

"Readers will be rapt by Abdelmahmoud's striking ability to forge a voice that's both raw and tenacious. Hilarious and somber, introspective and rollicking, this search for self is breathtakingly original."

—*Publishers Weekly* (starred review)

Son of Elsewhere

Son of Elsewhere

a memoir in pieces

Elamin
Abdelmahmoud

BALLANTINE BOOKS
NEW YORK

A Ballantine Books Trade Paperback Original

Copyright © 2022 by Elamin Abdelmahmoud

All rights reserved.

Published in the United States by Ballantine Books,
an imprint of Random House, a division of
Penguin Random House LLC, New York.

BALLANTINE and the HOUSE colophon are registered
trademarks of Penguin Random House LLC.

Published simultaneously in Canada by McClelland & Stewart,
a division of Penguin Random House Canada Limited.

ISBN 978-0-593-49685-5
Ebook ISBN 978-0-593-49686-2

Printed in the United States of America on acid-free paper

randomhousebooks.com

1st Printing

For my parents, whose dreams I carry
For Emily, who lights my way home
For Amna, for your elsewhere

Yet I live here, I live here too, I sing,

SEAMUS HEANEY

I still care enough to bear the
weight of the heaviness to which
my heart is tethered.

BRANDI CARLILE

CONTENTS

Elsewhere

I am a student of migration stories. I am pulled toward accounts of lives rearranged by the journey from one place to another. If you tell me you are an immigrant or a child of immigrants, we are going to spend some time together because I will want to hear of the ways you've had to stretch yourself to find your footing.

Your story might include yearning for a home you haven't seen in some time (if ever); it might also feature the hard work of adjusting to new expectations. But neither the yearning nor the adjusting are the point. Instead, I am interested in the constant calculus of how much of yourself to allot to each homeland, and how you navigate the anguish that comes with giving one of them less. This is Elsewhere.

Elsewhere is the sharp contrast between the here and the there. Elsewhere is when you are compelled to note the differences in weather and temperament and attitude and air between a once-home and a now-home, just because you walked past burning incense that reminded you of another world.

Elsewhere is not a vast land, but rather a sharp edge you inhabit. It's identity as a volcano: Elsewhere is the hot, frothing outcome of two tectonic plates constantly crashing into each other. There is violence in this—two lands trying to outdo one another. But in the fissure there is also order: yes, there are earthquakes and tremors, but frequently there is a brief truce. Fragile compromise. When neither is raging for attention, you might find yourself teetering but steady, perhaps even recognizing the patterns of your sway.

Perhaps you pitch a tent in the dislocation. Perhaps you begin to recognize, then eventually categorize, what triggers feelings of insufficiency. Perhaps you take Hindi classes at night, or have a tattoo of a word you can't say in a language you don't speak. Elsewhere is an orientation, an emotional frequency, a chaotic compass that waits until you take a step in one direction, then immediately points in the direction behind you.

ONE

Son of Elsewhere

It took two stopovers and nineteen hours of total flying time for me to become Black.

I left Khartoum as a popular and charming (and modest) preteen, and I landed in Canada with two new identities: immigrant, and Black.

When the friendly customs agent stamped my passport and said, "Welcome to Canada," he left out the "also, you're Black now, figure it out" part. In retrospect, it would've been immensely helpful. Having lived twelve years as a *not* Black person—which is to say, a person entirely unconcerned with his skin colour—you can imagine it was a jarring transition to make.

Without an instruction manual, I was left to my own devices to figure this whole race thing out. And luckily,

I had one thing going for me: the place I had just moved to was one of the whitest cities in Canada. This was going to be *great*.

❤

Let me tell you some of the boring shit that made my eyes glaze over in history class when I was in Sudan. In the early nineteenth century, Muhammad Ali Pasha, an Albanian Ottoman military commander, was sent by the mighty empire to wrestle Egypt from the grip of French occupation under Napoleon. When Muhammad Ali succeeded, he was made Wali, or viceroy, of the Ottoman empire's newly acquired plaything.

Not satisfied with Egypt's resources and gold, the Wali commanded his son to lead troops into Nubia. As it turned out, plundering is mighty easy when you have an advanced army, so the joyride continued. The Ottoman troops rolled on south and seized the province of Kordofan. *Where shall we go from here?* they wondered. *Eh, how about east? Why not!* East it was, to take the Sultanate of Sennar, which surrendered without a fight.

Conflict forges identity, though, and the Ottoman audacity managed to unite disparate tribes that had little reason to unite before. Their union was the birth of modern Sudan, though it took its time gestating: in 1881, sixty years after the Ottoman troops invaded, the Mahdist Revolution exploded in Kordofan.

The revolt was named after the Mahdi, an inspiring religious leader who became its rallying point. An army of farmers and merchants and tribesmen, now under a relatively coherent collective identity, said, *You know what, enough of this.* And Kordofan inspired the other regions to join in the fight.

These regular people, armed with swords and spears and sticks, began a revolution against the occupiers. It concluded in 1883 with victory for the Mahdists, and Sudan became the first (and only) colonized African nation to expel a colonial army by force.

One tiny hiccup: by the time the Mahdists won, Egypt was a de facto protectorate of the British empire. Which meant Sudan had just de facto handed an ass-kicking to the mightiest army in the world. And empires de facto don't like that very much.

The British took a deep breath, gathered their wits, and in 1899 retook Sudan and demolished the Mahdist state. Then they established a new framework, whereby Britain and Egypt would rule Sudan together.

∨

The population of Kingston, Ontario, is estimated to be about 85 per cent white, which is another way of saying it's like *holy shit* white. Kingston is so white, way too many people say things like "my Black friend." Kingston is so white (*how! white! is it!*), it has a town crier who is not only one of its most recognizable faces, *he also won a title at the world championship of town criers*. Lots of Kingstonians know this fact. They will tell it to you at parties.

All of this is to say: Kingston is not the easiest place to settle as a new immigrant. It's not exactly a gentle introduction to a new land. It's for good reason that most new immigrants to Canada find themselves in a major metropolis—a Toronto or a Montreal or a Vancouver or (if you must) an Edmonton. The idea is, when you have more people who look like you, it's easier to recognize how a place can become home. By contrast, in Kingston the whiteness was overwhelming.

When we arrived in Kingston, Baba made a point of introducing us to the other Sudanese families. All in all, there were eleven families, a small constellation of people who looked like me and could speak like me and were, too, constantly aware that we were far from what we considered home.

I related to the parents better: their Arabic was still instinctive. I could talk to Sudanese parents in Kingston like we were running into each other in Khartoum. They had a muscle memory for the belly laughs and the *keifaks* and the way Sudanese greetings go on and on and on.

The Sudanese kids, welcoming as they were, tried their best to swish the Arabic words in their mouths. Their parents had told them to take it easy on me, so they collectively pooled all the words they knew and brought them to me as an offering. But I could tell that even though their parents had spoken Arabic to them their whole lives, and their homes were decorated with heirlooms of Sudan, they wore their Sudanese identity like a sweater that didn't quite fit. They identified with something else.

That something else, as it turned out, was Blackness. I found this out when I visited a cousin living in Toronto. She was effortlessly cool, and had arrived in Canada four years before I did. "I don't know why your Baba chose Kingston for your family," she said. "Over here, we're Black. And being Black in Canada is way harder in a place like your city. You'll see."

The words *over here, we're Black* rang around my head. Before I could ask the million questions that swirled in my brain (*Wait, what do you mean we're Black? Does it come with rights and responsibilities? Do I get a card?*), she handed me two CDs: *The Miseducation of*

Lauryn Hill and *Illmatic.* "You won't be around a lot of Black people," she told me. "But hip hop can help you connect to them.

"And if you want people to think you're cool, get a hat with a Chinese word on it. Also, your pants are too tight."

❯

The turning point of the war between Mahdist Sudan and the British troops was the Battle of Atbara in April 1898, when Herbert Kitchener's army defeated 15,000 Sudanese soldiers. The vanquished unit's commander, Emir Mahmud Ahmad, was captured and taken to Kitchener in shackles.

The scene was painted by Godfrey Douglas Giles, who often captured military scenes for the British Army. In the foreground, one of the conquered dervishes lies dead. Far in the distance, smoke fills the horizon. A stoic Ahmad is depicted holding his head high as Kitchener scolds him.

Five months after Atbara, the Battle of Omdurman effectively put an end to the war and declared victory for the British. Kitchener lost less than 500 men in that battle, but killed 11,000.

Satisfied that Sudan was under his control, Kitchener ordered the Mahdi's tomb blown up—so as to prevent it from becoming a gathering place for a future revolution—and the Mahdi's bones were scattered. When word of the tomb desecration reached Queen Victoria, she wept.

It was this battle that gave Kitchener his reputation of brutality—Winston Churchill was disturbed by the killing of the wounded in Omdurman. "I am not squeamish," Churchill wrote to his cousin, the Duke of Marlborough, "but I have seen acts of great barbarity perpetrated at Omdurman and have been thoroughly sickened of human blood."

In 1936, the British withdrew from Egypt but kept their forces in Sudan. For more than a decade after, Egyptian governments demanded that Britain accept King Farouk as king of Egypt *and* Sudan, but the British refused.

It took until Egypt abolished its monarchy in 1953 for Egyptian leaders to drop their claim of sovereignty over Sudan, leaving little justification for the British to hold on to it. Gamal Abdel Nasser, the heralded Egyptian hero, was said to have thought that Sudan was too poor and would be a headache for Egypt to govern. In 1956, Sudan finally became an independent state.

In other words, it wasn't until Sudan became a needy hassle, an albatross around the necks of its occupiers, that the country became free.

∨

A hat with Chinese lettering wasn't hard to find in the year 2000. It was a mainstay of the early-aughts hip hop scene, a period of time famous for a) utter corniness and b) the start of hip hop's ascendance from subculture to the dominant mode of pop music.

So, I got the fucking hat. I got it from the S&R Department Store, an iconic and now closed shop where you could find, basically, anything—as long as you didn't mind navigating the inexplicably dark corners and the vague asbestos vibes. Whatever you wanted, S&R had it. I am certain they had lights, too, but somehow every spot you browsed was shrouded in shadow, which made shopping there feel like a treasure hunt.

I picked out a black hat with Chinese lettering made of *metal*. This hat was to be my armour: *I can't speak English yet, but yeah, I'm* cool. The rest of the prescription was harder to swallow, however.

I tried to like hip hop, which was an attempt at buying Blackness. (*I'll have one (1) Black identity, please.*) But there was one problem: I couldn't see myself in it. I'd grown up in a conservative Sudanese home. I was as prim and proper as they came. So in the crucial years of hip hop's rise, I balked.

Actually, "balked" sounds meek. It sounds like I had some concerns and maybe I'd like to speak to the manager. In reality, I *recoiled*. I remember sitting beside Tyler and Martin in art class, and the pair, aware of my aversion to swear words and anything offensive, insisted on playing me some songs. First, they played me Dr. Dre's "The Next Episode," which ends with the iconic Nate Dogg imploring you to "smoke weed everyday." Then "Forgot About Dre," where the Doctor himself says "fuck y'all, all of y'all, if y'all don't like me, blow me." I inquired what *blow me* meant, and Martin took particular glee in explaining it. I *literally* screamed in horror, and Tyler fell over laughing.

Meanwhile, on TV, Ja Rule was being arrested by a dozen cops in the "Put It on Me" music video, and Sisqó was singing about women's underwear and how he'd like to see it. It didn't help much that the biggest rapper in the world, Eminem, was angry about his mom and talking about his bum on your lips.

In my corner of Kingston, the only place I saw Blackness was in the world of hip hop. And everything about my life in Sudan (religion, private school, wealth—pick one!) told me to run away from that world. So that's what I did.

You might wonder, reading this: *Hey, Elamin, if you didn't have a place in the commercialized Blackness being*

shoved down your throat, why didn't you look for a differ-
ent kind of Blackness? Ever heard of the internet? To that
I say—it must be nice to have the gift of hindsight. In the
early aughts, the internet wasn't as big of a place.
Moreover, I barely knew what the internet was.

I felt condemned to stand outside of Blackness the
product. And I didn't have access to alternatives. For this,
I would like to blame Ja Rule. Somehow, it feels like it's all
his fault.

∨

It's not like colonialism ends with a clean break.
Colonizers don't just slip out the back door and leave
you to run your own affairs.

The Anglo-Egyptian regime that gave Sudan its
independence also left a terrible little gift: internal
division. The British, who could relate to Arabs, and
Egyptians, who *were* Arabs, had governed the north
and south of Sudan as two separate regions. But upon
exiting, they carelessly agreed to combine the two into
one administration, to be run out of Khartoum. They
left the lighter-skinned, urbanized, Muslim people of
mixed Arab-African descent in charge.

Sudan's new government was met with calls to
increase the representation of people from Southern

Sudan, who tended to be darker skinned, more rural, Christian, and predominately of African lineage. But the Northern elites who made up the ranks of governance of the newly formed nation rejected this. They reasoned that the British had left them in charge because they were capable of it. They believed the story their colonizers had told them. What could go wrong—right?

The episode kicked off decades of violent conflict between the North and the South, and systemic discrimination against Southern Sudanese people in the majority of the North. The first civil war started in 1955, five months before Sudan became an independent nation.

It is possible to be born at war with yourself.

⌄

In truth, it wasn't just Ja Rule's fault. Part of the reason it was so hard for me to compute that I was now Black in Canada was because I grew up with my primary identity being Arab. We were Arabs, we told ourselves.

Khartoum prides itself on its contributions to Arab culture, from novels to singers to actors. Independent Sudan constructed its identity around Arabness, and access to the Arab world. The religion of the Northern elite, Islam, deepened Sudan's ties to other Arab and Muslim nations.

Though there are dozens of regional dialects, Arabic is Sudan's official language. Not that I knew any of this when I was twelve and living in Khartoum: being Arab was the water I swam in. I couldn't tell you what it was like outside of that water.

I rarely thought about my skin colour. I just didn't have to. I knew that my complexion came from the mixing between Arabs and Africans that had dominated most of Sudan's history. And I knew that my family had social standing.

The skin colours I did think about were those of Southern Sudanese people in Khartoum. *They* were "Black": their skin several shades darker than mine, they spoke Arabic with hesitation, and they were clearly not like *us*. So when grappling with the notion of being Black in Canada, this was my only reference point. *That's* Black, I thought to myself.

This designation, unshakable in my mind, carried all kinds of weight and connotations. Casually, we'd call Southern Sudanese people living in the North horrifying names like *abeed*, or "slaves." The elaborate racism of the Northern elites often excluded Southerners from the job market, from housing, from security. Though in reality they were economic migrants, tormented by circumstances specifically created by various governments in the North, the racist narrative I heard growing up was that they deserved their lot. That they were heathens for not becoming Muslims. They were unjustly blamed for thefts, rapes, murders, and every plague that haunted Khartoum. Occasionally, local governments would promise to end the flow of these migrants coming north.

In the midst of unrelenting racism, Southern Sudanese people worked low-status jobs with no security. Most often, they worked as *khaddams* (servants). Though theoretically these migrants chose the labour, in reality they were beholden to the families who employed them for economic security and, sometimes, living accommodations. You rarely saw a Northerner working as a *khaddam*. I overheard families speak of lending each other their *khaddam*: "Oh, I'll send my girl over to help with your wash," they'd say.

You might think we had one or two *khaddams* during the twelve years I lived in Sudan. I remember five. Four were a family—twins Sandra and Sally, and their two younger sisters, Kelly and Kristine.

Sandra was Mama's go-to. The oldest of the twins by four minutes, she occasionally lived in the separate room we had at the back of the house, sometimes for weeks at a time. Her day often started with sweeping the front courtyard, until Mama called her inside to give her another task.

On occasion, Sandra brought her sisters along for the work. From time to time, they'd set up the daybeds—extra beds we had for when it was nice outside—and they'd sleep in the courtyard or on the spacious balcony. Kelly was closest to me in age, just a couple of years older, and I found myself asking her to play often. Sandra would interrupt her work to give Kelly a glance, in what I understood later to be a warning not to get too comfortable.

Though I rarely had to think about my skin colour, I do remember one night that it was top of mind. When I was ten, after a particularly joyful evening of playing with Kelly, I asked Sandra if I could join the sisters in sleeping on the balcony. A cool breeze was blowing, and I loved sleeping outside on such nights—and besides, we weren't done playing yet.

Sandra hesitated, and Sally chuckled at her hesitation. I lay in one of the daybeds and looked over to see Kelly spread out on her bed, the moonlight a gentle silver beam on her skin. I noticed that her skin and mine did not glow the same under the moon: its beads pooled on her arms and gave off a gorgeous reflection. Mine absorbed the light, ate it all up, and gave little back.

As I began drifting off to sleep, Mama's voice punctured the laughter, polite but firm. "It's time for you to return to your bed," she said, in a tone that didn't leave room for negotiation.

"But I'm having fun, Mom!"

"*Now.*"

As I groggily left the balcony and headed to my room, Mama called back, "Have fun, girls!"

I could hear Sally's distinctive laughter at the awkwardness of the whole thing.

Years later, I remembered how the moon had kissed Kelly's skin. *That's* Black, I thought to myself as I watched Ja Rule. And I am *not* that. So I dug my heels in, and refused to believe there was anything for me in Blackness.

A world away, it was still the same graceless dance—bending, arching toward whiteness.

❤

The First Sudanese Civil War lasted nearly seventeen years. From birth until the time it was a moody teenager, Sudan, led by Arab-descent Muslims, was waging a war against Southerners, trying to assert dominance over them.

In this tumultuous adolescence of a nation, Tayeb Salih wrote what would become *the* Sudanese novel. In 1966, *Mawsim al-Hijra ilâ al-Shamâl,* or *Season of Migration to the North,* was published in Beirut, in the *Hiwar* journal.

The book tells the story of an unnamed narrator who returns to his village in Northern Sudan after years of study abroad in the West, eager to help with the building of the Sudanese nation. There he discovers a mysterious man, Mustafa Sa'eed, who has recently returned from England. We learn that, while in London, Sa'eed vowed to take revenge against the British for how his country was taken, and his vengeance was exacted through sexual conquest. Sa'eed left behind a string of broken-hearted white women who worshipped him, before finally marrying one—a toxic marriage that ends in her death and Sa'eed's return to Sudan.

The narrator and Sa'eed are drawn to each other, bound by their shared experience of having lived in the West. What unfolds between them is a meditation on colonialism and the way it looms in the psyche of the colonized—long after the colonizer has left.

Salih himself travelled to London in the early 1950s, before independence, as a kind of ambassador: he was part of the generation of Sudanese people educated in

Britain in preparation for the country to become its own master. He spent most of his life abroad, joining the BBC's Arabic Service. In 1965, a year before the publication of *Season*, Salih married a Scottish woman, Julia Maclean, and they settled in London.

Though Salih was fluent in both Arabic and English, he wrote in Arabic, often with a Sudanese dialect. He set his work in Sudan. Actually, he was much more specific: like with Faulkner's Yoknapatawpha County or Gabriel García Márquez's Macondo, most of Salih's work takes place in one fictional place—a village called Wad Hamid.

Edward Said, the prominent postcolonial scholar, said *Season* was one of the six greatest Arabic novels. In 2001, the Arab Literary Academy in Damascus declared it the most important Arabic novel of the twentieth century.

❧

But if not toward Ja Rule, then toward what?

I trained my ears to listen to how white Kingstonians talked. Not that I had much of an option: they were *everywhere*. I became a devout fan of wrestling because I overheard two students talking about how much they loved it. I listened to the rock radio station, because 1) they spoke like the people I was trying to mimic and 2) absolutely no Ja Rule.

I ran away from anything I saw as "Black." This extended even to my name. In early high school, I was volunteering as a stagehand for the school's talent show. After I set up the microphone incorrectly, one band's singer (hi Jeff!) apologized to the audience as he was readjusting it, and jokingly said, "Stan the Microphone Man set this up wrong."

For years after, everyone called me that. At first, it was the whole phrase. Then, gradually, I just became Stan. I began *introducing myself* as Stan. What a perfect escape vehicle—no one ever suspects a Stan to be Black. Right now, if you flip to page 76 of the 2004–2005 Bayridge Secondary School yearbook, you'll read in my graduate goodbye that "for as long as I live, I shall forever remember my real name, Stan the Microphone Man." *My real name.*

"Stan" was a gateway. It was an identity that manifested non-Blackness for me, which is another way of saying it approximated whiteness. "Stan" was the vehicle with which I turned away from the Blackness I saw on TV. Seeing Blackness on TV and then *nowhere else* meant that, for me, being Black in the West was an absolute, fixed thing, and I was not it.

But just because you want to walk away doesn't mean you can. It's not up to a person in a Black body to decide not to be Black. Just as Southern Sudanese people in Khartoum couldn't escape the meaning attached to their skin in that context, I couldn't escape it here. The Blacks of Sudan and the Blacks of the West carry the implications of their skin colour in the same way.

So Stan, the kid who listened to Linkin Park and watched wrestling, couldn't choose not to be read as at least a *little* Black. This came out in throwaway comments from white friends, like, "Well, you're Black but you're not *really* Black." The implication here was: *I recognize that your skin colour is dark, but you are not exhibiting the other symptoms I associate with Blackness.*

To be sure, I received "you're not *really* Black" as a compliment. I cloaked myself in the superiority of it. It made me feel good to hear this; it was a way to note the distance between me and what I saw as a negative force. Yes, Ja Rule and I shared the same complexion, but we were *not* the same: he was Black, and I was not really that.

What "you're not *really* Black" connotes is comfort. Sure, I look like this, but I could be introduced to your parents. White dads loved me because I spoke like they did, listened to the same music they did (Kingston's best rock, 105.7), and they didn't have to stretch any muscles to talk to me. We could bond over The Rolling Stones.

Oh, you're a Beggars Banquet *guy? I'm an* Exile on Main St. *man myself.*

There's a name for this: you're an *Oreo*—Black on the outside, white on the inside. The politics of being an Oreo are familiar to all the Black kids who have had to grow up in predominantly white spaces. All the elements that make up your everyday life, a life lived in proximity to white people, are used to demonstrate how "white" you are.

Here's the thing—I *loved* being called an Oreo. I relished the suggestion that somehow, beneath my skin, my internal workings resembled whiteness. This was a *win*. But this was not a new feeling. It was the same feeling of noting the difference between my skin and Kelly's skin, and realizing mine held power.

Under the same graduate goodbye in that same yearbook, among the slew of nicknames I picked up throughout high school, I proudly list it: "Oreo."

∨

One of Salih's greatest triumphs in *Season* is his success in pushing colonialism beyond a simplistic good/bad binary. And he does this by showing us the turbulent inner worlds that come with being colonized.

In London, Mustafa Sa'eed plays up his exotic appeal:

he is nicknamed "the black English"; he rigs up the lights of his home to present his dark skin in a sexy, mysterious light; he turns his home into a sort of shrine to Sudan, which entices the white women he is aiming to seduce. Yet when he returns to the village, he transforms his study into a shrine to the West, yearning for it. He moves between worshipping two worlds, though never the one he is in.

There's a name for this: "hybridity." The living in-between. It's a central concept to postcolonial studies, one developed by scholars like Homi K. Bhabha and Gayatri Spivak. Hybridity creates something entirely new—neither colonizer nor colonized, but eternally suspended, living in the liminal.

Sa'eed deploys language to assert his similarity to the British. His mastery of English is his "sole weapon," he says—a "sharp knife inside my skull." This happened in the schools the English built in Sudan, schools that were "started so as to teach us how to say 'Yes' in their language."

There's a name for that, too. It's what Bhabha calls "mimicry," when the colonized begin to copy the culture of the colonizers. It's a particularly powerful tool: "The menace of mimicry," writes Bhabha, "is its double vision which in disclosing the ambivalence of colonial discourse also disrupts its authority."

In other words, it doesn't mean you don't see that you're being like the colonizer. On the contrary, you *see it quite clearly* and you refuse to give it power. Mimicry is a survival tool. It's the invisibility cloak that lets you move freely without the pressures of the colonizer, without drawing attention to yourself as the colonized.

But if you're not careful enough, if you leave the cloak on for too long, you can vanish underneath it.

❯

It helped that I wasn't alone in my repudiation of Blackness.

The Black kids of the West made Mama nervous. On occasion, she would literally clutch her purse on the bus after seeing a young brotha with pants saggin'. And it's not like someone explicitly told her that she should fear them. It was telegraphed on the news and in TV shows. TV taught us how Canadians thought. It was an education in images.

From time to time, when the pop radio station would play a hip hop song, Baba would joke that this was "the music of the *abeed*." He was making explicit what I had already learned to carry in my head: that these songs were not our songs, that we were superior to those who sang them.

In retrospect, "pick up your pants" and "turn down that rap music" are highly unoriginal starting points; they are the basic tenets of Black conservative homes. You saw them at work when Will moved in with his auntie and uncle in Bel-Air. But to a young boy in Kingston, surrounded with few Black faces, they were delineations of where our family stood on the what's Black/what's not Black conversation.

The summer before high school began, Baba took me to my favourite Tim Hortons, by the train tracks. He bought me an Iced Cappuccino, and started to explain something very serious.

"Son," he began gravely. "You're about to start high school, which means you're not a boy anymore." Ah. So this was his version of The Talk. "And you should know: here in Canada, they see us as Black. That means white girls are going to see you in a certain light. Be careful."

My parents were not naive about the consequences of being read as Black. Baba's rousing speech about my transition to adolescence was . . . a *warning*.

∨

Everything I knew about being Black went out the window when I got to university.

In my high school graduating class, there were three Black students, including me. The school had ten Black kids in total. But just across town, on the campus of Queen's University, I met a whole new universe.

Queen's had more Black people than I had ever seen in Canada up until that point. And not just Black people, but people of all races—a kind of diversity I had never encountered in the suburbs of Kingston, just a few miles west.

Queen's has a reputation as a particularly white institution. But in the fall of 2005, to me, it might as well have been the biggest, most diverse metropolis on earth.

In my first week of university, I introduced myself as Stan. New people, new place, new contexts—where better to go full mimicry, skip the hybridity dance, and just complete the blending in, right? I felt a little part of me sting but a bigger part of me swell with joy every time I beamed and said, "Hi, nice to meet you, I'm Stan."

Occasionally, I got puzzled looks, and from time to time I'd clarify: "My name is Elamin but I go by Stan." Usually that ended it. The passing was complete. I didn't have to confront my ideas about Blackness because I was Stan, the guy who spoke English the way white Kingstonians do. My go-to party trick was sharing how long I'd been in Canada, and the fact that I'd just learned English a handful of years ago.

This trick, by the way, worked *every* time. Recognition that I was passing fuelled me, and when I deployed that ol' move, I got a decent refill. The faces on white people. "You speak English so well," they'd say. They meant: *You speak English like I speak English.* What a high.

It was all going swimmingly. Sure, I saw the Black faces around campus, but I didn't have to do the work of squaring these new modes of Blackness with my deformed image of what Blackness was. That is, until I met Chantel.

Chantel was the coolest person I'd *ever* seen. Wherever she was, she walked like she owned the place, and everyone in the room believed it. Every quality about her she possessed to an otherworldly extent: she wasn't just smart, she could end an argument with one sharp rebuttal; she wasn't just beautiful, she was stunning; she wasn't just fashionable, she had an undisputed elegance; she wasn't just brave, her bravery awakened something in you so that you too could be that brave. Her unmistakable afro bounced with an airy confidence because she knew who she was; meanwhile, the rest of us didn't even have the syllabus on how to figure ourselves out.

The first time I met Chantel, she walked right up to me, with the biggest smile on her face, and handed me a new edition of a small zine called *CultureSHOCK!* It was filled to the brim with prose and poetry and paintings of people whose names were mouthfuls like mine. They wrote about their skin, which was like mine, and their attempts to blend in, which were like mine, and their attempts to fight, which were nothing like mine. They strung together words that stung—words that laced my heart with a pain of recognition.

That day, Chantel held the zine in her hands, smiled, and said "Join us." I didn't understand then what a profound act of generosity this was; to see another person as a part of your tribe when they don't see themselves that way is an act of kindness. It requires that you extend yourself to another.

I'm not sure Chantel and I ever exchanged more words than that for the rest of my university career. But like the Baader-Meinhof phenomenon, where you notice something and then start seeing it everywhere, she became a constant. She was in the cafeteria, handing out flyers for an anti-racism rally. She was in the street, asking people to sign a petition to force the administration to hire more non-white professors. She was in the school paper, fighting the student government.

She was far from the only match, but she was the most visible match to me in the powder keg that was

Queen's University in 2005. I didn't know it then, but campus had a problem, and it was about to erupt.

Just a few months after Facebook became available in Canada, and *one* month after my first year started, a second-year student decided to dress up in blackface as Miss Ethiopia for Halloween. The photos quickly spread online until it became the talk of the campus.

But that particular racist shit was happening on top of a bigger problem: just a few years earlier, six faculty had quit the university, citing racism. Queen's had then invited Dr. Frances Henry, a professor from another university, to examine race issues at Queen's.

The Miss Ethiopia incident made national headlines just as the university was grappling with the extensive report, dubbed simply the "Henry Report." It found that only 117 professors out of 1,378 faculty members identified as people of colour and/or Aboriginal. Henry went on to point out a few other issues with Queen's: for starters, it had "Eurocentric curricula." But the big takeaway was that the university had a "culture of Whiteness"— Henry concluded that Queen's had an environment in which "white culture, norms and values . . . becomes normative and natural. It becomes the standard against which all other cultures, groups and individuals are measured and usually found to be inferior."

Wheeeeew. So you're telling me that the campus where I'm seeing more Black people than I have *anywhere else* in Canada actually *doesn't have enough Black people*? I found myself in the middle of a tempest over race, after years spent avoiding it.

Moreover, Chantel was surer than me that I was part of an "us." Her confidence was infectious. She seemed certain that there was room in the "us", even with my conflicts and questions about Blackness. She was so sure that it punctured through my unwillingness to think about what I was taking in. For the first time, I looked around and saw one million iterations of Blackness, as real as I was, staring back at me. Nerdy Black people and jock-type Black people and intellectual Black people and theatre-geek Black people and business-school Black people and law-school Black people and conservative Black people. Black people who came from cities and villages, from other ends of the country and from other continents. All the possibilities I'd associated with whiteness, stretched to encompass Black bodies all at once. Bodies that included mine, its place now obvious in a gorgeous mosaic of Blackness.

Through Chantel, and through a conversation about race so loud I couldn't tune it out, I learned that you can create a world so white, you cannot even see how white you've made it.

∨

The narrator of *Season* finds himself perusing Mustafa Sa'eed's study—a space with an extensive library and a fireplace and an office, styled like the study of a rich Brit. In it, the narrator discovers that Sa'eed appears to have authored a book. His name is written on the spine. It's titled *My Life Story*.

The book, however, is a lie: the pages are blank, save for the dedication, which reads: "To those who see with one eye, speak with one tongue, and see things as either black or white, either Eastern or Western."

This is who Sa'eed considers most important. Who he has dedicated his unwritten story to. He does not feel it worthy to write down the story itself; he just notes with precision the audience he considers most cherished.

And why shouldn't he admire those not caught up in what torments him? It's as though he is sick, offering his life story as a lesson for the well: *May this aid you in avoiding my disease, which I couldn't cure.*

The ailment is being colonized, and being convinced you like it. When you go too far in mimicry and can no longer tell what's true and what's just a lie for survival. The injury to the psyche comes when a colonizer creates criteria with which you can gain favour, and you don't just play by those rules, you believe in them.

Hurt people hurt people and colonized people colonize people, and I was no different. I began to recognize the same dynamic that had played out over decades in Sudan. The British had convinced my people— Arab-African mixed people—that they were worthy of ruling and judging and having power over Southerners, and we believed them. Here in Canada, it took me little time to identify the equivalent group, and aspire to the same superiority, without ever giving it a second thought.

❧

I became Black the way a person falls asleep: slowly at first, then all at once.

Black kids born in the West have their whole lives to wrap their minds around the identity. This is not to say it comes easy to them, if it comes at all—it's just to say that, by arriving later in life, I was at a bit of a disadvantage. I spent twelve years never thinking about it, and several more outright rejecting it, so they had a slight head start.

Being Black felt, to me, like a deliberate constellation of tastes and aesthetics and lineage, and I had no access points to them because I did not know the history. Blackness, after all, is a learned biography, a book you have to read, though some of us have only watched the movie. Living in a Black body is a starting point of inheriting Blackness, but there is a rich archive of thought, art, and politics to get caught up on.

It's further complicated by the omnipresence of American Blackness, and particularly the one-dimensional story of Blackness that dominated pop culture in the early aughts. This is, unsurprisingly, a Ja Rule problem, too: trying to take in the contours of Black life in Canada and Black art in Canada while tuning out the loudness of America's cultural force is nearly impossible.

Still, I had names to learn, events to memorize. Was there going to be a pop quiz on this stuff? Did I need to know Choclair's birthday?

I started with what I knew: words. Writers like Ta-Nehisi Coates introduced me to the way Blackness colours politics and economics. George Elliott Clarke gave a sense of history and place to Canadian Blackness.

But music is where it all started to sing. It became easier to look beyond Ja Rule, who, it turns out, was not the most accurate representation of Blackness in America. I had a bit of help here: I was lucky enough to be born in the time of Beyoncé, and my Blackness came of age as she dove deeper into hers. Talib Kweli and Mos Def filled in some of the rest of the picture. Kanye West did, too. I finally went back to *Illmatic* and *The Miseducation of Lauryn Hill* and got what I was missing. "Everything is everything," she told me, and it felt like a homecoming.

I listened to these artists, and when they referenced other artists, I wrote down the names. Every footnote led to another artefact. These rivers led back to the sources you'd expect: Toni Morrison, James Baldwin, Nina Simone, Langston Hughes, Muddy Waters. I spent time with artists who love Black people, who love being Black, who invest energy into the maintenance of Black history. "I arrived on the day Fred Hampton died," Jay-Z rapped, and onto Google I went to look up who that was.

What I was finding weren't just keys to understanding the puzzle of being Black in the West. They were tools for undoing the years of colonial thinking I'd been led to believe for my entire life.

❣

In 1989, a brigadier general named Omar al-Bashir gathered a group of his army friends and staged a coup, removing the elected Sadiq al-Mahdi from power. Al-Mahdi, the great-grandson of the Mahdi who had united Sudan against colonizers in the 1880s, was an intellectual who, before he was elected, published a book on how the Sudanese nation could resolve its Southern Sudan problem.

Al-Mahdi became prime minister in 1986 on the strength of a hard-won coalition of Northern-based parties and four small Southern parties. When he was ousted, he was in the middle of negotiations with rebels in the South to end a brutal civil war. Bashir saw these negotiations as a capitulation to an inferior South.

In the 1990s, Bashir's government attacked *Season of Migration to the North*. Their charge was that the novel violated Islamic teachings, with its depictions of sex and portrayal of Sudanese villagers drinking and engaging in various acts of debauchery. Though they never officially banned the novel, they pulled it from schools on the basis that it shows Sudanese people doing the haram things Westerners do.

I imagine it is hard to look at what we are, and what we can be. I imagine we cannot sustain an intimate look at the ways colonialism has left us deformed, and the ways we keep deforming ourselves in its name. I imagine it is hard to fix our gaze on the ways we are slouching toward whiteness, stooping, stooping, until the light of dignity fades.

Well into my career, a Black journalist told me I needed to make more enemies. This comment stayed with me because I didn't understand it at first—who would want more enemies?

Months later, it dawned on me that what she meant was that I needed to think about all the ways I make white audiences comfortable when I talk about race, when perhaps they *should* be uncomfortable. On the face of it, she wasn't wrong: as a journalist, my work is often addressing an imagined white audience, probably an audience of Kingstonians, to whom I am apologetic, deferential. In writing and on-air, when speaking about racism I often deploy the explanatory comma, and have a reserve of non-inflammatory synonyms at the ready at all times. This Black journalist was trying to get me to question why that is. Am I still hesitant to own that I am Black— still protective of an aspirational proximity to whiteness?

The short answer is "maybe." The long answer is that I am still discovering the ways I learned to hate myself.

∨

I read somewhere that Tayeb Salih had to reassert his Arabness in nearly every interview he did. In being feted, he was made into the singular image of An Author Representing Africa. But, of course, he was more than that. He wrote in Arabic because that was an indivisible part of his identity. To then be *celebrated*, but in celebration be reduced to a comprehensible identity, stripped of its range, was a profound irony.

It is the Arab part of the Arab-African hyphenate that resulted in decades of emulating white supremacy exacted on Black bodies. But it is just recreating the cycle again to choose to discard it. Best to confront it, bring it to the centre, and say: *Look, these are all my colours, and from them I will forge myself.*

African and Arab melodies have echoed through Sudan's history for thousands of years, but white people needed categories of who ruled over whom, and who should be the subject and who should be the ruler. This is the legacy of colonialism: it leaves you warring with yourself.

In Salih's novel, Sa'eed gives voice to the scene when Emir Mahmud Ahmad was brought to Kitchener in shackles after the Battle of Atbara. But it is Kitchener who commands the Emir to answer, "Why have you come to my country to lay waste and plunder?"

These people will take your home and then ask you why you're standing in their house.

❯

In a referendum held in January 2011, 99 per cent of South Sudanese people voted in favour of independence. The South officially became its own independent state in July of the same year.

When I asked Mama why we'd called Southern Sudanese people *abeed*, she cringed with her whole body. She told me the shadeism I had grown up with would make us backward people in modern-day Sudan, which is trying to move beyond such blatant racism.

What I am trying to say is: it is possible to reform your idea of yourself. It's the only real inner work there is—going back and revisiting your horrors, and holding yourself accountable and moving forward.

Living in Kingston, I was attached to an identity of specifically *not* being Black. But this thinking wasn't born when I landed in Canada. It was born when Muhammad Ali's son rode south to Nubia. It was strengthened when Kitchener ordered the destruction of the Mahdi's tomb. It was tattooed on me when the British left people who looked like me in charge—in the process, alienating me from people who were also me. And then it was made immediate when I arrived in Canada, looking desperately for whiteness, craving it—partly because, in Sudan, I'd had something that felt like it.

It is not your choice if your mind is colonized. But it is your choice to confront it. My diasporic wound is that I am still feeling my way around Blackness. Internalized white supremacy is not the n-word and the pointy hats; it's the wobble in your step, the doubt in the back of your mind.

I do not see with one eye. I do not speak with one tongue. It took two stopovers and nineteen hours of flying time for me to become Black. It took a years-long war with myself to realize I've never been anything else.

You cannot banish the ghosts from your past, but you can turn from them, flailing, and limping toward redemption.

TWO

Roads (Part I)

The first friend I ever made in Canada was the highway. Before the boy with the Xbox in one of the basement apartments, before the skater kids with the baggy jeans who let me hang around them in the schoolyard, before the Christian kids with toothy grins, it was the highway.

And it makes sense: I met the highway first. I met the highway when my emotions were raw and my confusion was high. I met the highway minutes after I landed at Pearson Airport to a small and boisterous welcome party—led by Baba, who I hadn't seen for five years. I met the highway while trying to make sense of how everything was about to change.

There's a great big clearing in the arrivals hall of Pearson Airport. Congregating people awaiting their loved ones always leave the clearing empty, until they see who they're waiting for. I suspect this is because everyone waiting has agreed to an unwritten contract: you have to give people space to let their emotions occupy the whole room when it's their turn.

Perhaps the man who hasn't seen his mother for years may need some breathing room to fall apart after feeling her touch again. Perhaps the wife who hasn't seen her husband for months may need a wide berth to leap, knowing she'll be caught.

The clearing is where the emotions live. Where people do what they need to do, and onlookers kindly avert their gaze. Where people leave their preceding loneliness or misery or anticipation and enter joy.

Me, I entered the clearing unknowingly. Mama and I passed a series of sliding doors in a magnificent maze of sliding doors. We couldn't read English, so really we were just following the crowd, who seemed to know where to go.

We exited the last set of sliding doors and, as the frosted glass parted, I saw Baba. And before I said a word, he began crossing the clearing, making his way through the holy space. He held my face in his hands for what seemed like an eternity, as though his brain was, in real time, replacing the photos he was sent from Sudan with the real thing. And I could see that his emotions filled the room.

He introduced us to our welcome party. Eight people, in three cars. All of them Sudanese people who lived in the same city as Baba—the city that was about to become home. They took turns telling me how much Baba had talked about our arrival, and how they'd worried he might crash driving to the airport because he was bursting to see us.

Between the fluorescent lights of the airport, the overwhelm of the welcome party, and the sudden realization that Baba really was right in front of me—not to mention the dawning reality that I would now call this place I just landed "home"—I needed time to process and get my bearings. Acclimate to my surroundings. What were we dealing with here, exactly?

Then my eyes filled with wonder as we hit the highway. It was the biggest thing I'd ever seen. If you'd lived your whole life in Sudan, a country plagued for decades by subpar infrastructure, you too would've marvelled at the way the on-ramp bleeds onto the 401, which in turn gracefully ducks beneath the magnificent winding arch of the 427 but is somehow still above Highway 27. You would've thought it was a miracle. The whole thing is a furious clash of snaking turns and exits, a geography of grace and chaos.

∨

The original plan was not complicated: Ontario needed a four-lane expressway that would link two of its significant borders, Quebec and Michigan. But the 401 was born out of new thinking in planning. Unlike the Queen Elizabeth Way, which runs *through* towns, the plan for this new highway was to bypass cities altogether, so as not to create unbearable traffic burdens. When the Toronto portion was finished, some drivers didn't know where to find it because it was so far north of the city.

A decade later, planners found themselves adding lanes to the bursting road, which ballooned to twelve lanes at its widest—still the busiest stretch of highway in North America. This is not a surprise. Highways, like all connections, make themselves indispensable. We find ways to flow toward each other.

E.G. Pleva, a prominent scholar who founded Western University's Department of Geography, told *Maclean's* in 1964 that the 401 was "the most important single factor changing the economic and social patterns of this province." He was not exaggerating: though it took three decades for the 401 to be completed, opening in sections, it took far less time for communities to spring into being alongside it. Toronto extended its limits northward and eastward, kicking off decades of sprawl.

The communities that bloomed beside the 401 grew into cities in their own right. Industries blossomed. A town like Stratford, famous for its theatre scene, suddenly found itself a full hour closer to culture-hungry audiences in the big metropolis. Meanwhile, small- and medium-sized universities that had once serviced a limited market could advertise themselves to big-city prospective parents as being just one quick highway ride away.

London—a bustling city in the sixties—was already growing at a fast rate. Its planners were ready for this, and had set aside hundreds of acres north of the city for the growth spurt. But "virtually overnight," notes *Maclean's*, "London's growth patterns switched to the opposite direction—the direction of the 401."

Like a sunflower, the city shifted and bent itself toward this life force. We propel ourselves outward—and with urgency, we turn to seek one another. It's just what we do.

❤

As we sped away eastbound on the 401, I was in awe of the order. Traffic in Khartoum had never been logical, with traffic signals serving as, uh, let's say . . . gentle suggestions. Each roundabout was a hurricane; each intersection a crowded royal rumble.

But here was the 401, both organized and mad. My eyes never stopped darting from one direction to another, trying to take it all in: the big trees, which even in the warm highway lights I could see were undeniably lush; the absence of people shouting at each other to get out of the way; the vast expanse of a road that went on and on and on. The first time I'd ever been overwhelmed by incalculable possibilities. *I live here now*, I reminded myself.

The car pulled off the highway for a Tim Hortons stop. I remember it vividly: the beigeness of it all, the ease of it all. I remember my jaw dropping when I heard Baba ask for coffee in English, signalling a whole world I hadn't yet thought about. *Baba speaks English!* It was like watching a magic show, and each sentence he said was a show-stopping trick. *What does* double-double *mean? Is this code for something?*

The feeling of being a newcomer and taking stock of a new life in a Tim Hortons feels like a supremely personal memory, something I and I alone went through. But seventeen years after arriving, the coffee chain released a commercial spot called "Welcome

Home." It shows a Black man, anxious and excited to meet his family at the airport after several years apart. You see his children dart across the clearing in the arrivals hall. You see the family's long embrace of relief. And after the man picks up his family, the first thing he does is introduce them to the iconic cup of coffee. I came to learn that The First Tim Hortons is as standard as going through customs.

But that day on the highway, my eyes just widened in wonderment at how much there was to learn. About this new land with its expansive roads and giant trees. About Baba, who could move in all of this so easily. About the ways a person could be. About what the hell a double-double was.

I had to sneak glances at Baba. Here he was: the man I had idolized in absence, made flesh. It was too much to take in, that this was actually happening, and I couldn't look all at once. First, a glance to see how grey hair now adorned his moustache. The greys had clearly made their home on his face some time ago; they were not recent migrants. But I'd never seen his face like this. And the round glasses! How come none of the photos he'd sent us in Sudan featured these glasses? At least I could've had time to get used to them.

I had grown up hanging on his every word, so finally seeing him after five years meant I had some catching up to do. I had to relearn the way he moved (with a newly hunched back), the way words wrapped around his tongue, the way he laughed with his belly (this was still the same). I had to relearn the tenor of his voice. I had to relearn the micro-expressions on his face, the subtleties of his hugs.

There is an intimacy to memorizing the lines on someone's face and knowing the way they walk. I had craved this for a handful of years—and now, faced with it, I was flooded and overwhelmed. With joy, sure; but also with the amount on the syllabus. I had some studying to do.

∨

The geography of the 401 doesn't vary much. It's lined with tall trees and farmland, and its vastness means that, as you drive on a flat road with gentle curves, suddenly a city comes into view, and suddenly it's gone. A town of 150,000 people can pass you by in four exits, then it's in your rear-view, and you're returned back to the trees. It's hard not to be romantic about this—a perspective of human life that lets you swing out wide and see a whole city, and how fleeting it is.

The genius of the 401 lies in the seamlessness with which cities bleed into ravines into farmland into little forests alongside. Within a five-minute drive, you can see all of these landscapes. This wasn't always the plan, however. When the 401 was proposed, conventional highway wisdom tended toward austere design. A road had to be functional: that was the main priority. It was unusual to suggest planting trees and rose bushes along a highway's shoulder.

But the Ministry of Highways believed that this planting would turn the 401 into a "thing of beauty to behold," which would maybe, possibly, encourage more responsible driving. They theorized that drivers would be so drawn in by the exuberant greenery and the stunning scenery around them, they'd slow down a little to take in the marvels.

∨

The first time I got to see the 401 in its full glory was also the first time I got to take in the Canada version of Baba in his full glory. A couple of days after our arrival, Baba made the announcement that we were going on a trip to see one of the country's wonders.

When you hit the 401 westbound in Kingston, it takes you three hours and fifty minutes to get to

Niagara Falls. It was a journey Baba insisted on: since we were going to make Canada our home, it was compulsory that we see Niagara Falls. Years before, when he arrived in Canada, Sudanese friends had taken him on the same trek, and here he was passing on the tradition.

We hit the road early, and let me tell you something about how the morning sun lights your way out of Kingston. It's majestic—the road gently curving around big limestone rocks, rising and falling with the whispering forests that line the way.

Baba was in his element: tour guide, steady sherpa in a land that was still foreign to us. But even more breathtaking than the land was the spectacle of watching him be so confident in this landscape. The last time I'd seen him, he'd had tears in his eyes. His spirit was shaken, feeling like he had to leave Sudan, pushed out by a government that had decided his politics were unwelcome. Now here he was, peppering his sentences with English words I didn't understand.

As the wheels of the van hit the highway, I let myself fall into full observer mode. From the back seat I could watch Baba, and take in who he was now. I didn't have to look directly at him; I could steal all the glances I wanted and get to know him that way.

And when I looked out the window, I saw the contours of a new home, and studied the lines of its face. I didn't have to think about the totality of the nation all at once. That would be an incomprehensible reality. I could just focus on these stretches that rushed by me. Love always begins in the specifics.

I have no memory of arriving in Niagara Falls. I have no memory of seeing the actual falls. In the photos I have seen from that day—photos mostly taken by Baba— I notice that I look happy to be there, but also bashful and overcome. I am relentlessly smiling.

I do have one memory of that trip: holding Baba's hand to jaywalk across the street. Holding his hand for the first time in five years. As cars zoomed by, he instinctively reached out and took my hand, and I melted, returning to a safety I didn't know I'd missed so deeply. I was perfectly capable of crossing the street by myself, but I held on tight. I do not remember letting go.

THREE

Infinite Reach

There is a song I remember from my childhood that occasionally gets stuck in my head. It's a simple song, a military chant that became ubiquitous in Sudan. Its opening couplet goes like this: *"Laikum y'almreekan / Laikum taslahna"*—"For you, Americans / For you we have armed ourselves."

We sang it as children, proudly, fervently, as though it was our arms lifting up AK-47s and our bodies running training circuits like the soldiers on TV. It felt personal. We had ownership over it. We, too, had armed ourselves.

When we sang it, we joined our index and middle fingers, resting our thumbs on top of the pair. We pointed toward the sky, shooting pretend guns into the air, our mouths emulating the sound of bullets.

❯

There was a cool breeze that August night in 1998. The power was out, but then again, the power was always out. Khartoum's power grid was constantly failing. My mother and I, we did what we always did when the power went out and we couldn't sleep: we took blankets and pillows, and went to lie in the beds in the front yard, making use of the breeze. Across the night sky, clouds were spread out evenly. Too evenly. In neat rows, like they were conspiring to hide something.

The signifiers of wealth shift in different contexts. In the context of my neighbourhood, an upper-middle-class neighbourhood, my family already had so much: a big house, a big yard, a comfortable life. But the ultimate marker of affluence where I lived was having a generator. If your family had a generator, it meant you weren't sentenced to the same fate as the rest of us. You could have AC whenever you needed it, and you didn't need to sleep outside or depend on the undependable breeze. The breeze in Khartoum in August is fickle. The breeze in Khartoum at any time is fickle. It comes too late, and never stays long enough. But wealth bought you the privilege to skip uncertainty. You didn't have to sleep in your sweat, or miss the newest episode of the Syrian drama on TV.

On our block, just one house had a generator. On the nights we all lost power, I imagined you could see their living room from space—one bright spot in an otherwise sprawling blackout.

That August night I was somewhere between awake and asleep, lying on the outside bed, when the conspiratorial sky let its guard down for a split second. I detected an object a little blacker than the night moving across the clouds. But when you're ten, you've learned to doubt yourself because adults remind you that your imagination is too active. *Did I just see that?* I asked myself, and before the word *Mama?* could escape my lips, the quiet of the night was pierced by loud explosions. Suddenly, the sky was ablaze.

It's hard to describe what happens when you think you're about to die. When there's danger abound, and your body is searching for a predator, feeling like this might be the end. The main thing I can tell you is that your reactions aren't rational. You might even look back and think they were insane. If you're lucky, you're not paralyzed by fear. Me, when I heard the explosions, I got out of the bed and I stood and stared at the sky, transfixed, immovable, awaiting another explosion, awaiting the end. I looked up and I froze.

Then I thought of my bicycle. My fire-engine-red bicycle with blue handlebars. I'd asked for the bicycle for two years, and finally, a few months prior, I'd got my wish. On that thing, I was faster than my cousins, faster than my neighbours, faster than the wind.

If this is the end, who's going to find it? What will they think of it? Will it be another kid like me? Maybe a grown-up, who'll give the bicycle as an Eid present to their nephew. Will he take care of it? Will he race his cousins, too? Perhaps he'll ride it to school to impress his friends.

All this went through my mind as I stood in place, gawking at the glowing night. Our house and our neighbours' houses were enveloped in a daunting darkness, their silhouettes rendered dramatic by the burning sky behind them. As I stared at the inferno, I could swear I saw the outline of a helicopter flying away from the fire. Now, a new fear: Did I just catch these invaders scurrying away from their mission? Were they trying to scatter undetected? If so, then had I just spoiled that? Surely, this meant I was going to die here, right now. I waited for them to strike me, specifically. One extra bomb, just for me.

And so I waited for death.

Mama, on the other hand, went into action mode. First, she decided to answer an immediate question: Is this still an active threat? Is there more danger to come? She put on her thobe and ran to the street. She surveyed the rising smoke as she stood talking with all the other mothers, who also seemed ready to fight someone if they had to. The block filled up with mothers talking to mothers, some only peeking out from their front doors to share intelligence.

In truth, I didn't know if Mama or the other mothers had a plan. All I could hear were murmurs from the street corner. *I was in the kitchen making ful by candlelight when . . . I was praying and suddenly . . .* or *I was doing the laundry and then.*

Everyone was confused. Had the civil war that was tearing the south of the country apart arrived in our suburb? The sound was really close, no more than six or seven blocks away, some said, their faces aglow with the fire that lit up the night.

All notions of sleep wiped from our eyes, Mama and I were invited in by the neighbours who had the generator so we could watch the news. There we were, five families piled into one living room, desperate for the television to tell us something, *anything.*

The wait for information seemed like forever. The whole time, the adults were debating who could've done this. "It had to be *Amreeka*," chimed one. "No, this is

Israeel," said another. Israel was always going to be on the shortlist for something like this—so went the logic.

I scanned the living room. The neighbours probably had cold Pepsi because their fridge was still running. I remembered that this was the same living room where I'd had my first kiss, not long ago. Come to think of it, the power had been out that night too, when Najma suggested we play house, and then . . . *Focus. Why are we here?* Oh, that's right, the sky is ablaze.

We got our answer. Bill Clinton, calm like the American men I had seen in the movies, calm like a man who hadn't just woken up a ten-year-old boy with an explosion, looked into the camera and said "Good afternoon," and then paused. Americans are so polite about these things.

"Today I ordered our armed forces to strike at terrorist-related facilities in Afghanistan and Sudan because of the imminent threat they presented to our national security." The English-to-Arabic translator told us what the president was saying. Silence fell over the room. We racked our brains—what was six or seven blocks away and presented an imminent threat to America? The only thing I could think of was a grocery store. I didn't like their bananas.

The operation was dubbed "Infinite Reach."

❯

Clinton's target turned out to be Al-Shifa, a pharmaceutical factory in Khartoum, not far from where we lived. Al-Shifa, literally "the Healing," was the pride of the country. It had officially opened in July 1997, and in its single year of existence the factory managed to supply 50 per cent of Sudan's medicines. The destruction of the factory left us without a supply of chloroquine. For the uninitiated, i.e. those who have never had malaria, chloroquine is the standard treatment.

Malaria in Sudan is quite common, as is its treatment. In poverty-stricken regions, malaria kills. Everywhere else, it's not unlike getting the common cold: when it's the season, your turn comes, you suffer a little, you take the medicine, and you're back on your feet in four or five days. I'd estimate that I've had malaria no fewer than a dozen times.

It meant a lot in the national consciousness to have a homegrown provider of the medicine we needed. We could heal ourselves, which meant we didn't have to beg other nations to cure us. We could tell the story of how we cured ourselves. I pretended to understand the significance when older cousins talked about it with pride as they gathered to chat politics.

But whatever pride we felt in Al-Shifa was levelled by thirteen Tomahawk missiles that August night. Cruise missiles aimed at a newfound source of dignity. Even Frantz Fanon would think that was a little too on-the-nose.

In America, people who didn't have to watch the flames take over the sky went into debate mode, mulling over the consequences. *Hmmmm, was this justified? Was the intelligence solid? Could it have waited a week?* To them, this was an idea to mull over, not an act of destruction.

That is, if they paid attention in the first place. It was a Thursday, after all—and in 1998, Thursdays belonged to NBC. As the flames burned in Khartoum, the network entertained millions of Americans with a stellar lineup of *Friends*, *Frasier*, and *ER*. Talk about heavy hitters. That night's *Tonight Show* guest was Neve Campbell. She was on to promote *54*, which also starred Ryan Phillippe and Salma Hayek.

The No. 1 song in America that week was Brandy and Monica's historic collaboration "The Boy Is Mine," and Spice Girls and Backstreet Boys were rocking the radio. The No. 1 film in America, for a fourth consecutive week, was *Saving Private Ryan*. There were bops on the airwaves, there were movies to see, and the nation was abuzz after Ross said "Rachel" instead of his actual bride's name. Who had time for the news?

The U.S. government's position was that the strikes were a necessary response to Al-Qaeda's bombings of the U.S. embassies in Kenya and Tanzania—attacks that killed 224 people. The U.S. claimed the facility levelled in Sudan was part of Osama bin Laden's sprawling empire of terror and functioned as a chemical weapons site. This turned out to be almost certainly not the case: CIA analysts would go on to say that the evidence linking Al-Shifa to chemical weapons was weak.

Curiously, the Clinton administration defended itself by suggesting that, although the intelligence was not a slam dunk, the attack absolutely had to be launched during a small window of time, as if the factory might grow legs and go into hiding. This tiny sliver of an opportunity, this unmissable time frame, just happened to align with the ten-day stretch when Monica Lewinsky, then Clinton himself, were to appear before the grand jury of independent counsel Kenneth W. Starr, who was investigating the Lewinsky affair.

Any reasonable observer would conclude that the chances of this fortuitous timing for President Clinton being a coincidence was, uh, highly improbable. I, not

being an impartial observer, would say it was hella suspect. But don't take it from me, take it from Christopher
Hitchens, who wrote that Al-Shifa "could not have been
folded like a tent and spirited away in a day or so . . . Well
then, what was the hurry? . . . There is really only one
possible answer to that question. Clinton needed to look
'presidential' for a day."

If you look like me, here is something you understand internally, before you're ever told: in America,
when presidents need to look like they're doing *something*, they take it out on Brown and Black bodies.
When governments need to look like they're in control,
they exercise that control over what can be subdued,
and that is often places where our bodies exist. Those
bodies—my body, and the bodies of my neighbours—
are vulnerable to the whims of America, to the needs
of insecure men. They understood this in Iraq in 2003,
when a reeling America needed to look powerful. They
worried about this in Iran in the late 2010s, when political commentators casually suggested that an erratic
president's path to legitimacy lay in waging war. It is
often Brown and Black bodies that bear the cost of
America's assertion of strength. We are the canvas
for brutality.

This is the real meaning of Infinite Reach. The

unfathomable extension of America's wrath—so broad and sweeping, that hemispheres sit in fear.

In announcing the strike, Clinton said that "the long arm of American law"—what a phrase—"has reached out around the world and brought to trial those guilty..." and that statement makes me want to scream in indignation. A trial by whose laws? As if we don't know the answer: the laws of Infinite Reach.

∨

When I was five, I had a weekly ritual with my father. Every Friday night, after Mama went to bed, Baba and I would open the door to the backyard to let the breeze blow into the living room, where we lay on two beds that were side by side. We watched *Walker, Texas Ranger*, completely in the dark. He had tea, and I was allowed to have an extra Pepsi. We watched Chuck Norris administer justice, with great ease, to demonstrably bad people. The satisfaction of the breeze and the satisfaction of the Pepsi and the satisfaction of Baba's company melded with the satisfaction of watching Walker kick some ass, and created my version of perfection.

The show wasn't dubbed. Instead, it was subtitled. Which is fine if you can read, but look, I was five. So I had to make do with Norris's stern face and quick gun and the menacing expressions of the bad guys. It didn't matter that I couldn't understand, because I understood. Walker dealt with black-and-white morality, where the bad guys were bad and the good guy knew exactly what to do.

One night we were watching Walker, the sound of TV bullets filling the living room, when we heard trucks pulling up outside our house. A knock came, and Baba got up to answer the door with an anxious look on his face. I could see shadowy figures talking to my father for what seemed like an eternity.

When he came back, in the flicker of the television light, I could see Baba's sullen expression. The shadowy figures, it turned out, were members of the security forces of the authoritarian regime. Baba owned a publishing company, and one of the magazines it distributed was *al-Dastoor*, the official publication of the now-exiled opposition party.

The government had ordered the publishing company closed, and the shadowy men were at our home to tell Baba that he was to shut down business the next day. They also seized the keys to his truck, a beautiful blue Toyota that I loved to pretend to drive. It handled the muddy road to the farm where I spent the weekends better than any other car. As Walker drew his gun on TV, in the distance I could hear the distinctive engine noise of the truck starting up. Then I heard it drive away.

Back then, I didn't understand who the shadowy men were, but I understood good men and bad men. And I understood what was supposed to happen to bad men. I turned to the television, then I turned to the door, and I waited for Walker, the Texas Ranger, to walk in. I waited for him to make this right.

❯

Where I grew up, people talk about moving to America like they might talk about moving to heaven. Those who manage to move, their families talk about them with indescribable pride: "He's in *Amreeka* now," they say, and then let the silence speak volumes.

That's because *Amreeka* means a problem has been resolved. *Amreeka* is an all-encompassing answer. *Amreeka* doesn't describe a place; it describes having *made it*. Made it where? The next part is never spoken out loud, but the answer is *anywhere that's Not Here*.

Not Here is, of course, a magical notion. It's what you need it to be. It's where life is sacred and not fragile, where the price of bread is not subject to the whims of a dictator, where electricity is bountiful and continuous.

Where they obey traffic laws, and there's never been a penicillin shortage. Not Here, where they have answers to every question.

America occupied such a large place in the imagination of the people I grew up around that there was hardly any room for any other nation. Cousins plotted and planned—"One day, when I win the lottery and go to America, I'll bring the whole family. And I'll send two hundred dollars every month until I can bring you," they'd promise. There was a sense that America could complete you. Almost as if to say—if you were going to leave home, why bother going anywhere else but The Place?

This is not at odds with living under threat from America—it's the other side of the same coin. If America has the capacity to destroy whenever it feels like it, logically the place that's safest from America's wrath is America.

Few speak English, but everyone can say "green card." It always sounds like salvation.

∨

"Almost heaven, West Virginia." So begins John Denver's "Take Me Home, Country Roads." The song is as perfect as they come, nostalgic and penetrating. It's universally likeable. There's a good chance you're humming it now as you read this.

But the thing about "Country Roads" is that it almost said "Almost heaven, Massachusetts . . ."

Bill Danoff, who wrote the song with his wife, Taffy Nivert, had never been to West Virginia before writing it. It was inspired by a road they drove on while on their way to Maryland, which is a funny way to spell West Virginia.

The pair played the song for Denver, perhaps as a test audience, but their plan all along was to sell it to Johnny Cash, because really, who could be more American? Cash never heard it, though, because Denver was smitten by the tune and its, well, Americanness. The story goes that he stayed up all night with the couple, rewriting and moving lines around.

By the time he recorded it for *Poems, Prayers and Promises*, with Bill and Taffy singing backing vocals, it had taken the form we know now, a form built on little bits of deception. And that makes sense: if West Virginia came to supplant Massachusetts in describing a road in Maryland, why not play with the rest of the song, too?

Geography nerds and literalists know that the Blue Ridge Mountains and the Shenandoah River—the first landmarks invoked in the song—aren't exactly geo-graphically synonymous with West Virginia. Much of the river is in neighbouring Virginia, save for a brief dip into West Virginia. Meanwhile, the Blue Ridge Mountains only overlap with one of West Virginia's fifty-five counties. In other words, the associations are loose, more of a spiritual thing—more of a vibe than an actual location. But because of the song, the mountains and the river are now inseparable from the state.

None of this, of course, diminishes the song: it's not about a place, it's about geography as a manufac-turer of feeling. "To the place I belong," Denver sings, and you know what he means because you, too, have a place you belong.

Before every home game at West Virginia University, the song about a road in Maryland that was almost about Massachusetts is performed. In 2014, the West Virginia Legislature adopted "Country Roads" as an official state song.

Denver, a California-based artist for most of his career, understood that in order for the song to be about America, it didn't have to be too precise—that America is not bothered by specifics. Which is to say it was suffi-cient for the song to *kind of* be about America. A rough sketch would do.

America is, ultimately, this dislocation. It's a vague idea, occasionally rendered comprehensible by the feelings it evokes. It has to be vague, because if you stare too long, the fractures become apparent and the feeling is lost. Up close, the fault lines appear. From afar, it's almost heaven.

∨

I struggled to stay awake in July 1994, waiting to watch Brazil play Italy in the FIFA World Cup final. My uncle complained that he didn't understand how America had ended up hosting the World Cup. "They don't even like football," he said bitterly. "They call it something else."

This made no sense to me—football only had one name—but I decided to adopt his frustration. "Yeah," I piled on with vigour, "they don't deserve it!"

It was, in fact, hardly a matter of deserving. The American bid to host the competition was victorious in 1988, earning ten out of nineteen ballots from FIFA executives. Morocco, the runner-up, ended up with seven, and Brazil managed two.

But it's where the votes came from that is worth noticing: the ballots were split down geopolitical fault lines. The U.S. snagged approval from Mexico, Guatemala, Turkey, Trinidad and Tobago, and all five Western

European nations. Morocco, meanwhile, secured support from the six African and Asian nations, plus the Soviet Union.

One additional, crucial, vote went to the U.S.— Hungary. In 1988, Hungary was in the nascent stages of ending communist rule, and its vote for the American bid was seen as a symbolic turn away from the Soviet Union.

That America should host the World Cup was, in 1988, an odd proposal. The 1984 Summer Olympics in Los Angeles had shown there was modest interest in football matches, but football was not a serious sport in the U.S. It was nearly forty years since the country had last played in the World Cup. The country didn't even have a professional national league.

Morocco, on the other hand, had sentiment and momentum going for it. Just two years earlier, it had become the first African country to top a World Cup group. It also would've been the first African and Arab nation to host. How could a tournament that is supposed to encompass the world exist for six decades and never set foot in Africa?

Nonetheless, FIFA awarded the World Cup to the U.S., with an executive cheekily noting that he was thrilled the American presentation had managed to call the sport "football." There were some conditions, though—for one, the U.S. had to actually establish a goddamn professional league. This is literally how Major League Soccer was born in 1993: it looked tacky for the U.S. to host the biggest tournament in a sport while boasting zero professional teams.

Halfway across the world, and several time zones over, I was yawning as Brazil's squad took the field at Pasadena's Rose Bowl stadium to battle against Italy. The stakes were high—not just because it was the final, but because the previous World Cup, in 1990, had seen the Italians exit via penalty kicks in the semifinal, while they were the host nation.

And to add to the drama, one of the game's biggest legends, Argentina's Diego Maradona, had been sent home from the competition after just two matches because he tested positive for a performance-enhancing drug. His dismissal hung over the rest of the competition. "They're out to get Maradona! This would've been a different story if he was playing," I heard the grown-ups shout nearly every game.

But despite the high stakes, my investment was uncomplicated: I was in because this was the biggest stage of the world's game—the sport I played a few times a week with people I loved. Football bound us together.

That summer, I loved sitting in the living room, listening to the arguments. "Germany's defeat was a fluke!" and "Listen, the Dutch are going all the way, have you *seen* the way Bergkamp plays?"

If you were a football fan in 1994, you knew Romário's name. The way he slid past opponents like they were not there was the talk of every group of boys huddled on a stoop. Because of Romário's firework displays in that tournament, there was a consensus in my family to cheer for Brazil in this final. Naturally, I leaned toward the underdog and rooted for Brazil to lose in an ugly defeat. So when Roberto Baggio missed his penalty kick and handed the Green and Yellow their fourth World Cup title, I was furious.

But as pandemonium swept the Rose Bowl, I was fixated on the TV screen. It dawned on me that, for the first time, I was looking at actual Americans instead of imagining them. The shots of the crowd were my introduction to what Americans really looked like. And by and large, they looked . . . happy. Everywhere the camera went, ecstatic people were smiling and shouting. And why shouldn't they smile? As far as I understood it, they had everything at their disposal.

"It means nothing to them," my uncle said. "They just saw poetry on the field, and it means nothing to them." With despair, he said to no one: "And we'll never see a World Cup in Africa, where it belongs." You learn early that America takes what it wants, when it wants it.

❧

In the summer of 2014, I convinced three friends to get in a car and make the twelve-hour drive to Nashville, Tennessee. For them, it was a road trip. For me, it was a pilgrimage.

The truth is, I wasn't sure what I would find when we arrived in Music City. But I had long felt a pull to be—just *be*—in the South. I had, and still have, a deep romance with the American South. I've been drawn to the art that comes out of the South, particularly country music and the ways it centres lineage and history. I had absolutely no proof that Southerners were my people, but I was sure of it.

And boy was I right. The lights of Broadway, the twangs pouring out of every bar, the easy demeanour of Southerners who seemed so happy to meet you. We ate extraordinary feasts in backyards lit up by fireflies. I danced so much it put a hole in the bottom of my shoe. In a boisterous, narrow honky-tonk, I thought the second floor was going to cave in as we all foot-stomped and shouted about way down yonder on the Chattahoochee.

On our trip, we weaved in and out of joy, in and out of brutal history. We visited a Civil War cemetery and stood below a colossal Confederate flag, beside the names of hundreds of soldiers who had fought to keep people who looked like me as slaves.

I stumbled upon an elaborate mausoleum. Next to it, a sign explained that this tomb belonged to a woman who was one of the few merchants able to keep selling cotton during the Civil War. She became massively wealthy. We wondered if her great-grandchildren felt good about the wealth that was passed down to them, and how it was won.

I had thought this pilgrimage would satisfy my hunger to experience visiting the South, but in fact it unleashed a larger curiosity about travelling America via road trips. Flying is robbing yourself of a journey—you merely apparate to your destination. A road trip forces you to fill in the blanks, and confront the spaces you can ignore from 20,000 feet.

Since that summer, I've gone on a road trip every year with those friends. We've embarked on a mission of filling in the blanks—making real the places we'd only imagined or seen in movies. We went to Boston, and found ourselves on Bunker Hill. We went to Pittsburgh, and I still have no idea why. We drove to Philadelphia, and got deliriously, deliciously lost. We went to Columbus, and met the kindest people. But the real point of it all is sketching a clearer outline, not just of our destinations but also the places that lead to them. When we can, we take the long way home. Returning from Philadelphia, we took a circuitous route through the Appalachian Mountains. It was almost heaven.

Since that first road trip, I've had to confront an annoying fact: I love America. I really do. It's an uncomfortable fact for me, this love. It cannot be divorced from that August night in Khartoum, and the piercing memories of America administering destruction near my home and injecting fear into the hearts of people I love.

But the pull is there, always—the magnetic force of romance. I felt it acutely in the passenger seat heading south down the I-65. It is definitive and inevitable. The closest approximation I can get to explaining it is that it seems eternal, undisputed. And that itself is a kind of reach. Through country music and through movies and through Great American Novels, this idea has burrowed into my brain that The Answer, regardless of the question, beckons. That the American open road and the feeling of finding yourself in a Great American City is itself a prayer answered, a cleansing light on that which ails you.

I am intelligent enough to know that this feeling is manufactured, and yet gullible enough to still believe it, because the sunsets in Coen Brothers movies are always perfect and deep. I can only surmise that this enduring gullibility is the product of omnipresence: I grew up with America casting a long shadow over my life. It was both the lurking malevolence and the saving grace. Being this close to it is intoxicating.

We do things out of fear and we do things out of love and no one tells you what happens when you act from both places at once. America is a mystery to me, and I am yet to unlock it. Say the word, and I'll hop in the car with you. I'm still trying to figure this out.

❯

Laikum y'almreekan. That song about arming ourselves creeps into my life when I least expect it. The last morning in Nashville, I woke up early and headed out for a walk. On that quiet, beautiful morning, I walked into a church and sat in the back pew and listened to the service. I may not be Christian, but I like the idea of worship through essay, which is essentially what a sermon is.

The priest laid out his argument. It was something about love, something about fate, something about how no one on this earth is born before their time. Something about how all the things that have happened in your life are God's way of steering you to his house. I smiled and thought of how horrified my mother would be at the prospect of me sitting in a church.

As I walked out into the sunlight, I found myself humming that tune, "*laikum y'almreekan . . .*"

I thought of the last time I was in Khartoum, arriving late in the night, and as the car packed with family turned off the roundabout, I could hear Lil Wayne's "Lollipop" blasting from the car next to us. I looked to a cousin, confused. He said all the Sudanese youths listened to now was American hip hop.

Just then, I turned my head to see we were passing the site where Al-Shifa once stood. Today, the wreckage stands—the government has demanded an apology from the U.S. for the bombing of the factory, and until that happens, the ruins are kept intact, preserved as a memory of an injustice. A symbol that says *this is what they think of us.*

It's incongruent, the relationship between the love and the rage, but they need each other to survive. America's capacity for reach encompasses all of your emotions.

And I come from a place where America is both paradise and horror. I come from a people who have turned a wound into a monument, waiting for an apology that will never come.

FOUR

Wrestling

I race home from school on a Tuesday afternoon. Yes, there's homework, and I can't ignore it, but the reality is: it's not going to get my full attention. Not today. In about twenty minutes, I dispense with both the history *and* English assignments, because honestly, my heart isn't in it.

I am focused on another obligation. Tonight, at midnight, is the deadline for submitting a short piece of fiction. It's written in the first person, and it describes the life of a professional wrestler. But it's not for credit or grades; it's for glory. It's for all the glory. Tonight, if I do this right, I will be crowned World Heavyweight Champion of a small e-fed.

An e-fed, or e-federation, is a collective of wrestling enthusiasts who get together to write what is essentially fanfic about their favourite wrestlers. It's 2002, and I'm a member of four e-feds—and in this one, Xtreme Efed Championship, my title shot is *tonight*. I've put in months of work to earn this chance, and now it's here. In order to win, I have to write a world so elaborate that it takes the judges' breath away. It's a tough panel of experienced e-feders who've been around the game for years. There can be no room for error.

The minimum word count is 2,500 words, but I am already at 3,300. My fingers are racing over the keyboard, creating my universe, describing fictional training routines and pre-match rituals, inventing selves with each stroke. When the deadline passes, I will have to see if what I've created is good enough for the title belt.

∨

I got into wrestling for the same reason anybody gets into anything: I was an outsider who wanted to fit in. I overheard fellow students talking about how much they liked wrestling, and they seemed like the *cool* guys in school, so I decided to give it a go.

What's nice about the WWE—or WWF, as it was known at the time—and its brand of "sports entertainment" is that it really doesn't ask much of you. It asks that you cheer for a person, and buy into the idea that their opponent is the bad guy. It's a simple distillation of all the drama of humanity in the form of exaggerated vignettes, which are then settled with an elegant ballet of violence. And sometimes with tables and ladders and chairs (*oh my!*) aimed at backs, chests, legs, and necks.

The smack talk is a limited part of the theatre, so wrestling was particularly ideal for someone like me, trying to learn English. See, watching *Friends* wasn't on the table because I'd have to actually know what they were saying. Not so with wrestling. If I didn't know the few words being traded, I'd simply wait for the crowd reaction in order to ascertain that I was cheering for the hero and booing the villain.

What little dialogue I did pick up was not exactly helpful. For instance, I spent my first winter in Canada occasionally climbing atop snowbanks, spreading my arms as wide as possible, and shouting "RAAAAAAAVEEEEN." Do not do this. It is, it turns out, a highly unusual thing to do.

But watching *Monday Night Raw* and Thursday's *SmackDown!* became my first shorthand for an identity at a time when I was searching for one to silence the "immigrant kid" alarms that I imagined sounded in the heads of the white kids I talked to. These alarms may or may not have *actually* existed, but they were real to me—I believed that to each new person I met, the fact that I was an immigrant was the most immediate and therefore central truth about me. Wrestling gave me a fallback option: *I'm not foreign, I'm a wrestling guy! All the cool kids like it!*

It did not occur to me at the time that wrestling wouldn't make me cool—because, in fact, *not* all the cool kids liked it. I was too busy memorizing quotes from Stone Cold Steve Austin a.k.a. Austin 3:16 a.k.a. the Texas Rattlesnake, or learning Triple H's entrance-music lyrics.

But what liking wrestling *did* do for me was bigger than "cool." It made me my first friends in Canada: Tyler and Judd. Tyler was a scrappy kid who loved Green Day and skate shoes, and Judd was a prototypical film nerd. You wouldn't necessarily see them being close friends—or, for that matter, people who watched wrestling. But they'd grown up a few streets apart, and their friendship stretched from childhood. They were casual fans of WWE. And, for some reason, they let me start hanging out with them.

Tuesdays and Fridays were the best days: it was so easy for me to strike up a conversation with them on the day after WWE aired its marquee shows. I didn't have to reach for more than a few words. Just a simple *Did you see the Hardy Boyz* . . . or *I knew Chris Jericho would* . . . or *The way Mick Foley* . . .

Months into life in Canada, I still hadn't invited any friends over to my home. Not because I didn't want to, but because the very thought made me sick with anxiety. After all, I was trying to blend in with my peers, but if they came over, they'd really know the extent to which we were immigrants. I felt like it would be a burden: not only did my friends have to contend with my accent at school, in my house they'd also have to put up with my immigrant parents. If I didn't invite them over, I could at least forgo one more reminder that I was not from this place.

But in March 2001, there was an opportunity I couldn't pass up. WrestleMania.

And not *just* WrestleMania—WrestleMania X-Seven, with the main event being a long-time-coming match between Stone Cold and The Rock!!! On the undercard: The Undertaker vs. Triple H, and Kane in a triple-threat hardcore match against Big Show and Raven. This card made my mouth water.

I begged Baba to buy the pay-per-view. He shot back that we already paid for TV, and it was preposterous to pay more for TV on top of the TV you already paid for. These were, admittedly, good points, but I was relentless and after a while he gave in. I invited Tyler, Judd, and Judd's twin brother, Max. Seven months after moving to Canada, here I was on my way to making friends like the Canadians did: they were actually going to *come over to my place*!

Mama made me do all the cleaning that day. "They're your guests," she told me. I sneakily hid the prayer rugs and prayer beads, and cautiously tucked away Mama's bright green Qur'an. Embarrassing pictures of when I was eight or nine adorned our walls, but I couldn't do much about those. The walls of the condo were petal pink, and there wasn't much I could do about that either. But I could control the snacks. As I got the place ready for visitors, I steadied myself: yes, I was anxious, but WrestleMania would do most of the talking. Chips? Check. Giant bottles of Pepsi? Check. Spinach dip? Ready. Let's get this party started.

We all stared in shock as Stone Cold aligned himself with the WWE's CEO and most enduring villain, Vince McMahon, to defeat The Rock and become the new champion. It was a heel turn no one saw coming, and we couldn't stop shouting "holy shit" for fifteen minutes after it ended. As I went to bed that night, I revelled in the fact that the event had gone perfectly. For a few hours, between the crunch of the chips and the bubbles of the Pepsi and the *crack* of the bodies onscreen, it was as though no one in the room, not even me, had to think about the fact that I was an immigrant. This must be what belonging feels like, I thought.

∨

In Khartoum, the wealthy neighbours had a computer and the internet, but we didn't, so I vaguely understood what the internet was, but thought it was a thing for rich people, a thing I had no use for.

Upon arriving in Canada, suddenly the internet was readily at my disposal—aaaaaand I still had no use for it. Mostly, I went on the internet once every few days to watch the Arabic-dubbed version of *Pokémon* on the website of an Arab TV channel. That was the extent of my surfing.

Then along came wrestling. As my interest in WWE grew, I actually had a destination to visit on the World Wide Web: WWE.com! Man, the *fun* that awaited me. I could wander over to the WWE's website and read interviews with Kurt Angle and watch clips of Big Show. I could even look at pictures of Trish Stratus, though I had to leave the mouse hovering over the big *X* just in case my parents got close. And beyond the WWE website, I now had a use for the rest of the internet, too—through Ask Jeeves and AltaVista, I could get more into wrestling history. Now *that's* what the internet could do!

I was a studious kid, and suddenly I had all this information at my disposal. So I gobbled it all up. I printed and organized binders of information. One binder contained biographical details of every wrestler: their real name, ring name, birthday, and finishing move. Another housed the names of every WWE Champion, in order, along with amazing trivia details like the first champion (Buddy Rogers, 1963) and longest reigning champion (Bruno Sammartino, 2,803 days).

My most prized binder contained all the wrestling terms you needed to know. Like a *face* is a heroic guy, written to be the good guy. Turning *heel* means becoming a villain. *Putting over* means helping a character land with the audience. A *jobber* is a wrestler whose job it is to lose, to make another guy look good. So you might say, "Kane is no jobber, but when he loses to The Undertaker tonight, he'll put him over for his big face turn."

I didn't *have* to memorize these terms. I could've spent that time memorizing the difference between alkali metals and alkaline earth metals. I suspect my science teacher, Mr. Gorman, would've appreciated that more. But the heart wants what it wants, and my heart wanted to protect the knowledge that The Undertaker's real name is Mark Calaway.

The WWE.com chat room was where the internet came alive for me. I would get home from school, have a snack, and disappear into conversations with other *marks* (adj., a fan who buys into the scripted storylines and emotions of wrestling, and discusses them with joy and vigour). At first, I mostly watched the chat stream, but then I began offering my own opinions. I found liberation in the text-based medium: I was without an accent, and therefore without judgement. It was just me and the written words. In this world, I felt an unbounded freedom. I could try to make others laugh, and hold on to every precious *lol* in response. I could even dabble in a little cybersex—by which I mean take it to the direct messages, where I'd tell girls *I wanna give you an organism*. Girls love organisms.

The chat room itself became a portal to new online possibilities. I struck up easy internet friendships with people who had no idea what I looked like or how I spoke, only that we shared a love of Chris Jericho and Edge. And as friendships deepened, we could graduate to the next stage, the paragon of intimacy: MSN Messenger. There was Adam from Windsor, who always lol'd at my jokes at a time when I thought *lol* meant he was actually laughing out loud. And Melanie from Chatham, the first person to show me the value of asking "How was your day?" and debriefing about it for a minute.

Melanie would message me the minute my status said I was online, and we'd talk until one of us had to go to bed. Occasionally, we'd webcam and watch *Monday Night Raw* together. There were no organisms involved, okay? It wasn't like that.

After months of logging on every night, and practising communicating my thoughts and feelings in English, I realized that wrestling, which had given me my first friends in Canada, was also giving me community. Real intimacy. We were eager to share our lives with each other—prompted by twice-weekly televised events, but also because we were genuinely invested in one another.

One night, Adam excitedly popped up on MSN Messenger. "Elamin, do you wanna join an e-fed?" *Uh... what's that?* He explained that he was a part of this *thing* where you pretend to be a wrestler, and write a role play (RP), and others in the e-fed judge whether your RP is better than the other guy's. They were a group of seven, and needed one more to even it up.

"Who would I be?" I asked. Adam said he was Chris Jericho, and I could either be Edge or The Undertaker.

Easy. I'd like to be the Dead Man Walking himself, who had so much drama already built into his persona.

"What do I have to do?" I asked. The answer: write a scenario of how your character might prepare for his upcoming match. It could be anything. It could be a speech he delivers, or a description of his day building up to the match. The one thing you couldn't do was write the match itself. That's up to the judges. *Cool.*

❤

The black Ford F-150 pulls into an empty parking lot. Its driver door flings open, and The Undertaker leaps out. It's a rainy morning, and the birds are not yet awake, but this morning 'Taker is not taking his chances: there's work to be done, and no time to be wasted.

"Hey Jimbo," he greets the doorman of the gym.

"'Taker, good to see ya! Aren't you a bit early today?"

"Yeah man, but that punk-ass Jeff Hardy has something up his sleeve, and I gotta be ready."

'Taker seems cool on the surface, ready for the big day. But underneath, he's all nerves. This is the first match back in the ring since his shoulder injury eight months ago . . . the doctors said he'd never wrestle again, but the doctors didn't know they were dealing with a man who can't be killed. The Rock couldn't end him. Kurt Angle's arm bar couldn't end him. And he sure as shit wasn't going to tolerate the headlines and rumours that Jeff Hardy's

cheap shot with a ladder to the shoulder was going to be the end of him.

As he lifts the 45-pound dumbbell off the rack, he thinks about a headline he saw the other day: 'Is it time for The Undertaker to retire?' His face transforms into a sea of quiet rage. He knows that Jeff Hardy is half his age, and he knows what the headlines will say if he doesn't pull this off. He puts the dumbbell back, pauses a moment, and picks up the 60-pound dumbbell. "I ain't dead yet, motherfuckers," he mutters.

⌄

I studied up on the nuances of the roleplaying universe. The basic idea is that RPs are creative takes on the scripted interstitials you often see in a wrestling show. Those scripted "backstage" moments heighten the drama of what happens in the ring. In an RP, you write elaborate backstage scenarios, and based on how well you develop your character, the judges decide who wins the match. In other words, e-feding is like a short story competition for people who would never enter short story competitions.

Fantasy wrestling predates the internet. The world of wrestling-as-entertainment, with its biblical "good vs. bad" archetypes, is an ideal vehicle for role play. Part of the joy of watching is imagining what it would be like for 25,000 people to chant your name as you triumph over evil.

In the 1980s, one of the ways you could participate in fantasy wrestling was the play-by-mail model. You had to pay to create a character, and either preselect from a series of moves or allocate points to a fictional wrestler's abilities. You might have 100 points to spend, and you'd have to use those points to give your character more grappling abilities, or speed, or size, or whatever. Fans would then pay to enter their character into a match, and a judge would mail every participant a copy of the match's actions and results.

But then email arrived in the early 1990s, and it suddenly became much faster and more interesting to do fantasy wrestling. You could have the results back within two days! Email changed the nature of the fantasy, too—instead of limiting yourself to the abilities of your character, you could give them life, build a story around them. Inject some swagger.

By the mid-nineties, with the explosion of message boards, the process was seamless and democratic: everyone submitted their work in full view of everyone else, and you could have near real-time interaction. This was the prototype of what became the e-fed world, an organized ecosystem of fantasy wrestlers who came armed with a dream and a half-decent typing speed.

The first e-fed match I participated in, I lost. The Undertaker was up against The Rock, and I waited anxiously for the judges' decision to go up. "The Rock, by disqualification," the result read. In an e-fed, the judges have the job of writing out the match, blow by blow. After your RPS are submitted, they comb through them and incorporate elements of the stories into the match write-up. They describe everything that happens in the fictional ring, in great technical detail.

I learned that a DQ win means the judge wanted to acknowledge that the RPS were even in quality, and therefore the winner only won on a technicality in a close contest.

Each e-fed sets the number of RPS you submit per match. Some require you to tell your whole story in one RP. Others set the bar at four or five RPS—each a short story describing how your character is preparing for this match. I learned that e-feds that have a three-RP minimum (or higher) are *serious*, and e-feds that have a one-RP minimum are just fucking around. Two is the sweet spot. Two says: invest enough time to show us your craft, but also we understand you might have a life outside of the e-fed world.

I started getting praise for my RPs, and occasionally winning matches. And the more matches I won, the more time I spent on RPs. I joined more e-feds and staggered the deadlines: Online Championship Wrestling on Tuesdays and Thursdays; Killerz Efed Championship on Mondays and Wednesdays; Fucked Up Entertainment every other Friday. I was essentially a full-time RP writer, and a student on the side. When I wasn't writing scenes about Booker T or Shawn Michaels or Triple H, I was studying the craft of others, examining the ways they structured their stories and elevated their prose.

A couple of years into the e-fed world, I'd put in my 10,000 hours. I was invited to a new tier of e-feds, the one for serious e-feders, when Adam introduced me to XEC—Xtreme Efed Championship—of which his character, Mason Sadness, was the newly crowned champion. At this level, you didn't just copy the gimmicks and personality of an existing WWE character. No, you were a *pro* now. You had to make up your own.

At first, I was intimidated. These guys had rigid rules. They always did three RPs totalling 8,000 words—though you were free to distribute that word count over the three stories however you liked. Each e-feder had their own Angelfire page where their RPs lived. For each RP, they created a brand-new layout from scratch using more-advanced HTML than I could do. They created elaborate and ornate banners with impeccable Photoshop skills, using images of existing wrestlers with newly created names.

They got descriptive with their characters' backgrounds and wrestling styles. Mason Sadness was a grappler; his finisher was an elbow bar; his brother died in the Korean War; he'd never forgiven himself for not intervening when his father was killed in an armed robbery. These kinds of traits and wounds animated every RP. The character creation went *deep*. I had to get on their level—and fast.

Being an awkward immigrant kid, I decided it was best to avoid mining myself for a character. Instead, I created Taylor Stanton—a composite of two students at my school, Taylor Leblanc and Matt Stanton. I picked those two because they had something I didn't: ease in whatever space they entered. Taylor and Matt could walk into any room and all eyes would turn to them. Their jokes never missed. Girls blushed at their shrugs. They had the effortless charisma that I desperately pined for.

So I started listening closely to their conversations at school for witty and hilarious phrases, noticing how they carried themselves. The way they landed their jokes.

How Taylor accentuated his words with just the right amount of hand gestures. How Matt leaned against his locker carelessly, and how this simple act would get every girl's attention. I spent my days blending into the background, making mental notes; and later, when I got home, I used their phrases in RPs, and described their body language to convey cool. I was a thief—briefly adopting their bold personalities.

Taylor Stanton, my character, came from a working-class background and was the manager of a local gym in the Midwest. The gym was a stepping stone to his dreams: to one day be XEC champion, and prove to his dad that he wasn't just wasting his life.

∨

A flight attendant gently nudges the sleeping man. "Mr. Stanton, we'll be landing soon, and Mr. Ross would like to see you." Taylor grumbles something and unbuckles his seat belt. "Would you like a glass of wine before we land?"

He shakes his head. "No drinking on match days," he sternly replies.

Taylor looks out of the airplane window as the mountains of Utah come into view. "You could get used to this, huh?" a voice booms from behind him.

Taylor answers without turning around. "With all due respect, Mr. Ross, the private jet life is for you, not for me. Are you going to tell me what we're doing in Utah?"

James Ross, the owner of xec, grins mischievously. "Where would the fun be in spoiling the surprise?"

Taylor purses his lips. "I don't like surprises," he shoots back.

As he descends from the plane, Taylor is confused. "This isn't the Salt Lake City airport. Where the fuck are we?"

Jim grins even wider. "Welcome to the farm, son."

Taylor spots a familiar face on the tarmac. Stacey Miller, Jim's right-hand woman and the reason Taylor joined xec in the first place, is standing next to Lyle Thomas, the greatest xec champion of all time and Taylor's inspiration. "What the fuck is going on," whispers Taylor.

Jim hugs Stacey and shakes Lyle's hand while Taylor stands quietly. "His first time at the farm," Jim laughs.

Lyle nods with familiarity and adds, "I think the first time you brought me to the farm, I thought you were going to have me murdered."

"Same here," offers Stacey.

Taylor, agitated at being the only one not in the know, repeats himself, louder this time: "What the fuck is going on?"

Stacey begins to answer but Lyle steps up. "Allow me. Son, it's a pleasure to meet you. I've been watching your work and I'm impressed. Jim here thinks you're the future of xec. I think he's right, but you're a little ... green."

"Green?" Taylor begins angrily. "Listen, I didn't come here off the street, Stacey found me after I built a name for myself and—"

"Down, boy," chimes in Stacey.

"No, listen, with all due respect, champ, I—"

Lyle interrupts this time. "You're what? A fast brawler who could run circles around the kids in Des Moines? Listen, kid. You got moves. You're creative. You can think on your feet and squeeze out a win. But your footwork ain't shit, and you leave your left side open when you grapple."

Taken aback, Taylor goes quiet. Jim smiles again and says calmly, "If you're going to be the future of the organization, you're going to have to be the best damn fighter we have. These aren't the minors anymore, son. I brought Lyle here to work with you because we both see in you a future champion. You have to do what he says. Everything he says. The farm is where I make champions. But you gotta lose that attitude because there are ten guys waiting to take your spot. Whaddya say?"

❯

"Elamin did not engage with the material," the note at the top said. I got a bad grade in a history class, and bad grades meant I had to have an annoying conversation with Baba.

I came home and showed the grade to my parents. Baba was disappointed, and gave me the by-now standard line: "What's the point of us being in Canada, away from family in Sudan, if you're going to get grades like this?" I pretended like this line didn't bother me, but I never got around to forming a callus against it: it always pierced my teenage armour.

It was shaping up to be a bad day.

Feeling broken, I disappeared into the internet, and checked the next week's lineup in several e-feds. Then I landed on the home page for XEC, and there it was: "Taylor Stanton def. Simon Saber." My heart was pounding as I read the match description. The judges had written a twist: Jim Ross came out before the match and ordered that its rules be changed to those of a First Blood competition, and after a tense bout, Taylor body-slammed Simon into the announcers' table, splitting his forehead open.

I walked around my room for fifteen minutes, not knowing what to do with myself. I waited for Adam, who always logged on MSN half an hour after I got home. Sure enough, within minutes of him coming online, the message popped up: "Holy shit, dude!!!!!! You're champion!!!!"

I was ecstatic. In a field where we were measured by the worlds we created, I was the *champion*. The reward was to see your name up in lights, which is to say every time you opened the page for XEC you would see it right there on the front page: "Taylor Stanton, current champion. Reign: 3 days." Your name would remain there for a whole week, until the next match day, when someone else was given a shot to outwrite you.

E-feds and wrestling gave me permission to write and write and write until I was understood, and then keep writing until I was a *winner*. I wrote out my anxieties and fears on the page. And Taylor was a stand-in for my hopes—everything I wanted to be good at, he was good at.

With Taylor Stanton, I spent years in the e-fed world. I wrote hundreds of thousands of words and developed an elaborate fictional biography. Everything I overheard and spied in the real world that made me long to fit in, I baked into his character. While I struggled with my accent, he spoke with authority. He drove the coolest car on the block (a silver 2002 Toyota Celica). He held firm on his boundaries with his parents. Every fight I lost in real life, Taylor handily won in the RPs.

What wrestling gave me, I later realized, wasn't just a way to pass the time; it was a licence to expand beyond my real-life confines, a borrowed ease. A counterfeit world, yes, but a world in which my words mattered.

ⱽ

I left e-feds and wrestling the same way most people leave a hobby: gradually, you drift away from it, until you realize it's out of your life because it's not serving you anymore. Melanie and I never graduated out of MSN Messenger, so when that medium lost its urgency, so did we. Adam and I haven't spoken in years, though we give each other the occasional double-tap on Instagram.

But on occasion, I think of the comfort I have now in speaking to strangers, or the joy I get from having friends in my home. I don't take these things for granted—you wouldn't either, if you'd had to muscle your way into a language. I think about these things granularly, genea-logically, tracing them to their origin points. All the roads lead me back to the hours I poured into learning intermediate HTML to make my RPs more convincing; to the storylines I invented to heal my insecurities.

At an airport recently, as I was lost in some book, a little boy, aged about seven or eight, tripped over my foot when he was running. Without missing a beat, he got up and continued on his run. His dad, chasing behind him, stopped to apologize. "He thinks he's

Randy Orton or something," he said to me. I was surprised that, nearly two decades later, I immediately recognized a wrestler's name.

I looked over to see the boy, now delivering a speech to the suitcases before piledriving into his dad's coat. I imagined the story playing out in his head, in which he was the hero in a world where he had permission to invent. Perhaps it was about the stumbles of growing up, recast as a simpler tale where he could triumph. Or look, maybe he just liked to piledrive.

I gave the father a nod and a smile. And underneath my breath, I whispered to no one: "We've all been there."

FIVE

Roads (Part II)

Baba almost never talks about his first marriage. The one thing I know about it is why it fell apart. The two of them were living in Saudi Arabia when Baba's father got sick. He wanted to abandon everything—his work, his life, his friends—so he could go and be with his dad. She apparently disagreed. And that was that.

This is a story I think about when I consider how hard it must have been for Baba not to come home when Haboba, his mother, passed away. He had only been in Canada for a couple of years. Leaving would've meant jeopardizing his immigration status, essentially wasting the time he'd already spent away from Mama and me in order to secure a life in Canada.

Family has always been everything to Baba. He's the youngest of seven, and to hear his siblings tell it, he's also the one who got away with anything, in typical youngest-child fashion. It would've been easy for him, anyway: Baba is charming and gregarious and forges connections easily.

When Baba left Sudan, it wasn't to go to Canada. Initially, he went to Switzerland and claimed refugee status. But the Swiss turned him down, and soon after he found his way to Canada. He arrived without a plan, and started working night shifts at a convenience store. When I talked to him on the phone across continents and time zones, I'd ask him how he was, and he always had one answer: "Tired, but I can't wait until you're here."

By the time we joined him, he was managing his own store. He took me there the day after we arrived, and I watched him interact with the patrons. The customers loved him and the way he lit up with delight when he greeted them. They were curious about me, and I could only say "Hi," so he had to do the talking for me. "Is that your son?" they'd ask. "No, that's my dad," he'd answer, and laugh and laugh and laugh. He still gives that answer now. He still laughs and laughs and laughs.

The laugh that I remembered, that I was once again wrapping my mind around, was the key with which he'd unlocked life in Canada. His customers could barely pronounce his name, but they knew he could make them laugh. It was this dynamic that I watched the closest, and hoped to emulate.

I watched his magnetism at the local mosque, too. There, Baba is a reliable institution. After Friday prayers, semicircles of people naturally form around him. Dozens who may not know each other find themselves in conversation because Baba is at the centre of the group. His is a charisma that makes him the heart of any room he enters.

When we were in Sudan, walking with Baba through the neighbourhood meant stopping approximately every two minutes. Someone always wanted to tell Baba a story, or hear a joke, or check in with him. People naturally wanted to impress him. This often worked out for me because it transformed any ordinary outing into a special one, with little effort on his part.

I remember during an important football match for al-Hilal, the Khartoum club we support, he managed to convince the stadium security guards to let me sit on the ground in front of the players' bench. The team was losing 2–0, and I reached into the squad's cooler and helped myself to a cold drink. I fully believed Baba was magic.

That he ended up in Canada was, ultimately, an outcome of chance. When he realized Switzerland was a dead end, he'd been talking to some family friends living in Canada. They sold him on the idea. But it just as easily could've been family friends who lived in Iowa or Texas or Dubai or Oxford.

If Baba had ended up in any of those places, our circumstances would've undoubtedly been different. For instance, the family friends who live in Iowa run a McDonald's restaurant. In Texas, they're taxi drivers. But in Canada, Baba knew people who worked in convenience stores, and that's where he ended up, too.

But while the circumstances might've been different, it wouldn't have changed how focused Baba was on the mission: he left Sudan in search of a safer place to put down roots for his family. He sacrificed a lot to get there, and even more to stay there. He missed out on grieving his mother with his siblings to make sure it happened. He left a world where everyone wanted to impress him all the time, where he was the centre of attention in the neighbourhood, for a life of struggle and hardship.

But what does that sacrifice get you?

∨

A month into my first school year in Canada, all the eighth-graders were taken on a trip to see the Shaw Festival's production of *Lord of the Flies*. I'd been to theatres in Sudan but never to watch a play, so this was exciting for me—even if I was shaky on the material because I was shaky on the language.

We all piled into two buses and made our way to Niagara-on-the-Lake (three hours, fifty-nine minutes on the 401). We arrived to find that we would not be the only eighth-graders around. Plenty of schools had the same idea—and were here on the same day.

I'm sure the production was fine, though *NOW Magazine*'s review said the staging "shaves away many of the book's nuances and places good and evil in too heavy-handed an opposition." I didn't pick up on this because I didn't pick up on much—this was a play about boys my age, sure, but they spoke the Queen's English and I could barely answer "How are you?" at this point.

But a few minutes into the play, during the scene where the airplane crashes onto the deserted island, an impressive fake fire lit up the stage. As a hush fell over a theatre that fit thousands, overwhelmed by the sight of the fire I shouted, "It looks so real!"

I repeat, I *shouted* this. During a quiet moment. In a theatre of thousands. Please, end me.

Everyone heard. *Everyone* heard. We may have been near the back, but I could swear one of the actors turned his head. And our whole section of the theatre erupted in laughter, as a teacher explained to me that this is the part where we *shut the hell up*.

Not that she had to tell me. The reaction had already done the job. I watched the rest of the show in embarrassed silence, then boarded the bus quietly. And as the wheels turned back toward home, I imagined my flub to be the only thing everyone was thinking about.

As the rest of the class slept on the bus, I stayed up, anxious. *What must they think of me?* I'd been struggling to fit in *before* I made a fool of myself. I stayed up counting the cars we passed by or the trees that sped past the window—anything so I wouldn't have to think about the laughter. I stayed up until the bus's engine drowned out its sound. I stayed up until the highway lulled me to sleep.

⌄

Eastbound on the 401, just outside Belleville, there's a big sign that says "PAINT TEST STRIPS." It's yelling at you in all caps because you're about to endure a little chaos. It marks the start of a brief patch of pavement littered with seemingly random road-paint strips, the kind that usually signify medians or delineate lanes. But in this section of the highway, they are *everywhere*.

It's the portion of the highway where they try out road paint to see if it's up for the job. But they test it all over the place. The strips are strewn about carelessly. They are vertical and horizontal, and sometimes diagonal. They come in varying shades of yellow and white, and are never the same thickness.

In this stretch, traffic inevitably slows down. This is, in large part, because people panic. For a brief moment, it feels like you're driving on a highway of anarchy. Inexperienced drivers can lose their orientation and veer out of lanes.

For me, the strips are a timestamp. They tell me that I am forty-eight minutes from Kingston, and my heart begins to jump. The mess guides me home.

∨

In Grade 12, I somehow managed to convince my parents to let me go on the school's New York trip. Grade 11 and Grade 12 students were Big Apple–bound, and I desperately wanted to join them. So I sold Mama and Baba on the educational value of the trip.

I knew Mama and Baba would have reservations. For all of high school, boundaries had been a tough negotiation. It worried them sick that I would be so far away from them. It was my boldest act of pushing the boundaries yet.

After I packed and headed to the pickup point, I kept

waiting for them to change their minds. I thought surely they would. As I loaded my bag onto the bus, I looked for the familiar headlights. I imagined how the whole thing would play out: my mom would fling open the car door and shout, "Wait, that's my son! He can't go with you! That's not how we live!"

But the headlights never came. I boarded the bus, and as we slid down the 401, I felt my shoulders drop. This was going to be the furthest I'd ever gotten away from my parents' grasp—*Another country! No curfews!*— and as we picked up speed, I felt a new thrill.

There was, however, a problem: I had a massive crush on a lovely girl named Alice, and she was on this trip. Worse, she was three rows ahead of me on the bus. I spent the ride trying to catch her eye, to no avail. Still, that highway was witness to my butterflies. Me! In another country! *Sort of* with a girl I was mad crushing on!

I spent four days trying to muster up the courage to talk to her. The courage never came. What did come, though, was one chance to impress her. Before the trip, all the students got to pick two Broadway shows to attend. I, a wise man, picked *Spamalot* and *The Phantom of the Opera*. What a blockbuster itinerary. Go, 2005 me.

As it turned out, all of Alice's friends also chose *Phantom*, so in an act of stunning selflessness (my words),

I traded her my *Phantom* ticket for her ticket to *The Producers*. Did I want to see *The Producers?* No, I surely did not. Reader, I did not care to see Nathan Lane and Matthew Broderick in Mel Brooks's musical adaptation of the Mel Brooks film by the same name.

I *did* care to see *Phantom of the fucking Opera* on Broadway, the same show that would go on to become the first show to surpass *10,000 performances on Broadway* and become the longest-running show in its history. It's *Phantom*! It's what you go to Broadway to see!

But yes, Alice's smile intervened, and I wound up trading tickets with her and seeing *The Producers* instead.

I spent the whole ride back cursing the courage that never came. I contemplated saying something on the bus, wishing for the highway to give me strength, but I came up short. A week after we returned from New York, I called Alice without a game plan. I found myself saying, "I am calling to say I really like you."

After a long, awkward silence, the reply came: "Oooooh. Um. Thank you?" And that was that.

SIX

Running Down the Wing

It is always a profound act of generosity when one person carries the dreams of millions on their shoulders. What's more selfless than transforming yourself into a vehicle for the hopes of others? Mohamed Salah came out of nowhere and volunteered himself to realize the dreams of Muslims. Mohamed Salah rewrote the rules for how we were looked at.

When Salah picks up speed and bends and pivots and flies past a defender, it's all of us he's carrying on his back. He may not even know it, but it's something he does regularly. When Salah's left foot sent Egypt to the World Cup, he sent all Muslims to the World Cup, but he looked as calm as could be. He moves so easily for someone saddled with the weight of nations.

When a chorus of thousands sings his name in a stadium, it always feels surreal. I get panicky because I don't know what to do with this feeling. It resembles a lucid dream, so vivid and so unlikely that it forces you to be suspicious of your senses. But the story is so bold, I'd never dream of it. And it's really happening.

You must understand that Salah transcends the wildest dreams we had for ourselves. You must understand that Salah made it so they could see us and not see terror.

❧

In the world of music, the ostinato is the repeating motif. It is the constant, the ever-present, the calming recurrence. It persists, it endures, regardless of the way the rest of the action rises and falls. Think of, say, The Verve's "Bitter Sweet Symphony," and the way the strings act as the guard rails for your emotional experience during every measure of the song. An ostinato's job is to tether you to something stable. It's always there for you.

What was the first song you ever heard? The first melody to ever grace my ears was the first melody that graces the ears of many Muslims: it is the adhan, the call to prayer. Baba sang it in my right ear, minutes after I took my first breath.

But that's, of course, just the start of a recurrence.

From then on, the adhan is repeated five times a day from every mosque in town. Mosques amplify their call so everyone in the neighbourhood hears that it's time to pray. Except, in Khartoum, no one lives close to just *one* mosque.

We lived within a couple of blocks of four mosques, which is to say within earshot of four sources for the adhan. The easiest way to give directions to where we lived was like this: Take this major street north until you arrive at the big mosque, then turn right and keep going until you get one block before the next mosque. If you hit the green mosque, you've gone too far.

This meant adhans were the ostinato of my daily rhythm. The adhan for the Maghrib prayers at sunset meant that it was time to come home from playing outside. The adhan for the Isha' prayers meant there was half an hour before I had to go to bed. You could hear the adhan in every room in the house.

Sometimes, the neighbourhood adhans would start at the same time and harmonize with each other, as though they were a practised quartet. Sometimes they'd take turns, one waiting until the end of another adhan before they began. Calls to prayer are never meant as a competition—each one is issued as a warm invitation. Whoever performs the adhan usually does so in their best singing voice. It fills the air with softness and tenderness.

I no longer live within a chorus of harmonizing minarets. I most often hear the adhan emanating from Mama's phone, when an app reminds her that it's time to pray. When it bellows, she falls silent and lets the sound fill the room. Sometimes, in the quiet of the night, I close my eyes and think of the way people paused when they heard the adhan. I listen to the wind, fixating on the faintest echo of a memory.

∨

You cannot hear the adhan in Kingston.

The mosque in Kingston doesn't resemble any of the mosques in Sudan. In Khartoum, I was used to imposing exteriors announcing their presence, and decorated interiors suggesting not just care but lavish investment. In Khartoum, mosques occupy central real estate. Whole blocks are organized around a central mosque, with the urban planning emphasizing the roads that lead there. Minarets pierce the low skyline, like stars marking your path. When you get lost in a neighbourhood, you can find your way by knowing where the mosque is.

Save for a modest green minaret, Kingston's mosque looks like a skating rink. It sits on the city's edge, tucked in just off a lightly travelled road. To find it, you'd have to know what you were looking for. The first time my dad took me there, I thought he was turning into a school parking lot for a three-point turn.

Inside, the mosque is austere. The carpet is new, and the copies of the Qur'an are stunningly embellished, but everything else is economical, functional. The chairs are not especially comfy; the tables are school-cafeteria quality. And it makes sense that there is a focus on economy: the mosque is mostly funded by Kingston's local Muslim community—a little over three hundred families, total—and the purpose is to have a large space to congregate and celebrate and worship and mourn, even if it has to forgo the bells and whistles of mosques in larger cities, or the mosques in the countries we all once called home.

But who needs the bells and whistles when you've got joy? When I arrived in Canada, Kingston's mosque became a steadying force for me. It was where I met kids with names that were hard to pronounce, like mine. Some of them spoke English well, and some of them didn't, but what they all had in common was that me trying to learn the language wasn't a nuisance to them. We made fun of the sport North Americans call "football," even though some of them were born in North America.

During my first Ramadan in Kingston, we did the prayers together every night, then played while the adults finished up.

During the school week, I was busy creating a new story for myself, trying to blend in as much as possible. But on weekends and holidays, when I could tag along with Mama and Baba to the mosque, I felt like I was arriving in a neutral zone. At the mosque, I was merely a point along a spectrum of possibilities—second-gen kids who were born here or newcomers who'd just arrived, we all had a place. It was a gift not to have to perform.

Sometimes, Baba would make a point of arriving at the mosque before the adhan. "It puts me at ease," he'd say. If you weren't walking by the small speaker next to the front door of the mosque, you wouldn't hear the adhan. But inside the walls of the mosque, it would echo and reverberate. Inside the walls of the mosque, the melody briefly carried me home on its wings.

⌄

Fridays in Khartoum signalled the hardest decision of the week. Which mosque would I go to for the midday prayer? The answer had cascading effects: the choice of mosque determined which cousins I would see, which friends I would hang out with, which video games I would play. It also determined where I would debut new shoes or new pants or a new watch. The mosque choice set the tone for the rest of the day.

If I wanted to have an excuse to hang around the girl next door who I had a huge crush on, it meant going to the mosque that was down the lane and to the left. It was by far my least favourite mosque—their ceiling fans never worked and the imam was always surly. But I could walk home with my crush's brothers, and before you knew it—*oh sure, I'd love to come hang for a bit, I think I can fit that in.* I'm in!

On days when I wanted to see my cousins, I would walk four blocks and then make a pit stop at my aunt Jazz's house because she would always give me a Pepsi. Then I'd walk the last four blocks to the mosque by my uncle's house, and he worked for Pepsi, so that meant that after the prayer was done, you best bet there was going to be another Pepsi—so one mosque choice meant two Pepsis would drift my way without even trying. *Score.*

Sometimes I pretended that Mama "talked me into" going to the mosque halfway across town so we could spend time at her best friend's house after prayer. In truth, there were two boys who were close to my age, and they had a Sega Genesis *and* a Nintendo, so praying halfway across town meant a Sonic the Hedgehog marathon afterwards.

For Eid prayers and on major occasions, like before a wedding or prayers for the dead, we gathered at the mosque that bore our family name, Sheikh Khojali's mosque. It was by far the largest of the mosques I frequented, with a main prayer room and two overflow rooms. You could spot its minaret from several neighbourhoods over. Its adhan could be heard from miles away.

Sheikh Khojali's mosque was an extension of home for me. It was our family's base. It was, literally, my family's work: Baba's cousin was the imam. The best soccer pitch in town was directly beside the mosque, and it was the best because, on the hottest days, the mosque provided shade that covered half the field.

In Khartoum, Islam was an unspoken tether—prayers and mosques were connective threads that meant that, even if I didn't specifically intend to, I would regularly see everyone I cared about. It gave us ways to flow toward each other, without even trying.

❤

My first Ramadan in Canada was a bit disorienting. It began in late November, which meant the days were incredibly short and the sunset came early. This was good news—I didn't have to fast for very long, and the sensation of thirst paled in comparison to what it had felt like on the long, hot Sudanese summer days. I very much appreciated this part of the first Ramadan. Shout out to daylight savings time and the planet's rotational axis.

But fasting is just one part of the Ramadans I was used to. It had always been a month of connecting to family, and in Sudan that meant seeing them nearly every day. In Canada, the Muslim families did iftars together at the mosque . . . on Saturdays. That meant that I had to get used to a particularly isolated, insular Ramadan experience. No choosing which aunt I was going to visit today. No groups of people all watching the year's new Syrian soap that punctuated every Ramadan night.

But the hardest adjustment was the first Eid that followed Ramadan. For one, it had none of the style showing-off opportunities. In Khartoum, I spent weeks planning my Eid outfits. Eid was always a multi-day affair, and that meant I had to plan ahead. On the first day, the maroon pants. On the second day, my new jeans. It's hard work, okay?

My first Eid in Canada was in December. There is nothing cute or stylish about lake-effect snow in Kingston in December. It's just cold. The most stylish thing you could wear had to be buried under four layers, and it didn't even fit right because there was a thermal shirt under it.

And then there were the presents. The presents! In Khartoum, Eid meant every relative had something for every child. Occasionally, I had to make pit stops at home to drop off the haul from one relative before making the trip to the next. Eid meant the younger generation in the family was showered with love and attention and toys from just about everyone.

Mama and Baba tried their best to create an Eid vibe in Kingston. Mama baked her Eid cookies, and Baba arranged a get-together with the other Sudanese families. We laughed and we sang old Sudanese songs that I knew, and for a brief moment I tried to convince myself that the songs could take us back.

❖

On a bright Tuesday morning in September 2001, I was sitting in Mr. Caleb's guitar class, frustrated. We were learning Cyndi Lauper's "Time After Time." I'd just given up on the chord transitions. Going from a D-minor to a C was a near-impossible task for me and my stubby fingers. I'd never even held a guitar before.

I resigned myself to thumbing the bass part. It felt manageable, a steady wave of sparse notes that kept washing ashore. Maybe manageable and steady was a good way to start the second week of high school. Maybe I didn't need to learn the hard things all at once. Maybe if I kept playing this bass part, it wouldn't be obvious that I had no idea who Cyndi Lauper was, or what "Time After Time" was about.

But the newfound steadiness wasn't going to last long. Mr. Caleb told us to put down our instruments— "Gently! Care for the guitar, always"—and took us out of the classroom. We stood on a small staircase, awaiting instructions, as Mr. Caleb disappeared to the principal's office, and confusion reigned supreme.

It's amazing, the way information ripples through a pool of people, distorting with every new circle. By the time it reached us on those stairs, it was from a somewhat breathless kid who made it to school late. He'd heard something odd on the radio, something about how "Palestinians bombed America." Silence fell over the group.

As we waited for Mr. Caleb, another voice said, "I heard Arabs bombed a plane." A few heads began to turn toward me. "No, Muslims bombed a big tower." More heads turned toward me. "Arabs are Muslims, idiot!" "No, they're not!"

No one thought to give the confused kids some clarity. We were simply dismissed for the day, most of us puzzled by the bits of information we'd just learned. As I headed to my locker to gather my belongings, I could feel the hot sting of many eyes trained on me. Studying my face for a reaction.

I was one of a handful of Muslims in the school. Before, that mostly meant a raised eyebrow when I declined a pepperoni slice on pizza day. But now there was a new look, and I didn't recognize it. It would soon become familiar, but in the moment I was trying to place it. I didn't yet understand that it was meant to be connective—*hey, you're Muslim, the bad people who did this are Muslims, is this what you're about?*

None of us understood the extent of the carnage. None of us understood the way the world was about to change. But I understood that, in their eyes, I looked a little different now.

❯

Mo Salah is one of the most famous footballers on the planet, and it's impossible to impress upon you how unlikely this is.

He was born in Nagrig, a tiny Egyptian village about ninety miles from Cairo. Before he played in Europe,

Salah endured a brutal commute from Nagrig to Cairo to play for Al Mokawloon: four hours on four or five microbuses on the way there; five hours on five or six microbuses on the way back. He did this every day.

The reason we know this is because, as he ascended in the world of football and won trophies and broke records, sports journalists were tasked with recreating Salah's early journey. It's a juicy kind of journalism—white reporters on microbuses, knee-deep in the struggle ("Cairo gets up your nose and under the nails on your fingers. You can smell it on your hair and pick it from your ears," wrote one of the journalists who made the Salah pilgrimage). This is to say: Salah got so big, they wanted to walk ninety miles in his shoes.

When Salah scores a goal, he is dead serious. He runs to the nearest corner of the pitch, flexes every muscle in his body, and stands perfectly still. He does not smile. From time to time, he will raise a fist to the sky.

I imagine it's because, every time he scores a goal, he is thinking of the young Arabs and young Muslims watching him. I imagine it's because he is talking directly to us, drawing us out of ecstasy to drive home his point—that this is what we can be: triumphant, soaring. Through incredible displays, Salah might be suggesting, *we can beat back the image they've tried to pin on us.*

And the thing is: it works. In his home country, murals and posters and mugs and pins and sandals abound. A friend tells me that in Egypt they don't even say "Liverpool is playing today." They say "Salah is playing," as though it is just him in the stadium. And it may as well be, because he's the only one they watch.

They listen, too. After Salah recorded a PSA discouraging the use of drugs, Egyptian authorities reported that, in the first three days after its release, the number of people seeking treatment increased fourfold.

That identification with Salah is not just in Egypt, either; it's across the Muslim world. Twenty years after being involuntarily cast as the world's villains, we've produced a hero the planet can't stop watching. He belongs to all of us.

After Salah scores a goal and flexes every muscle, as his celebration is winding down, he kneels and kisses the dirt. When he does, the fans go quiet and let him have his moment of prayer. As he rises up again, the cheers explode.

For a split second, a Muslim man is praying on the pitch, and non-Muslim eyes are rapt in their attention, deferential in respect.

❯

I don't remember exactly when police cars started showing up at the mosque in Kingston, but in the months after 9/11, their presence started to become a constant. For a regular Friday prayer, it would be one police car. During Eids, perhaps two or three.

The official word was that they were there to help make the community feel safe. In the wake of 9/11, there was an uptick in hate crimes against Muslims. Women wearing hijabs were harassed in public. Mosques were defaced and attacked. Kingston Police's strategy was meant to be a proactive one: by making their presence known, perhaps they'd scare off any would-be threats.

I can't say if the strategy paid off. But what I can say is it didn't make me feel safe. It made pulling up to the mosque feel like you were exiting a demilitarized zone. It didn't help that we never saw the police officers themselves. I still have no idea where they went. Were they patrolling the perimeter while we prayed? Were they playing cards in the imam's office? The mystery only added to the tension I felt.

The khutbas changed, too, after 9/11. In their sermons, imams were forced to reflect the reality we were all experiencing. Topics like coping with racism became a mainstay, as leaders in the community worked to offer comfort. The mosque redoubled its outreach efforts—perhaps because it was the neigh-bourly thing to do, but more likely because it was hard and necessary work to refute the monstrous ways the media covered Muslims. I imagine someone has done the math behind this. I imagine someone knows the exchange rate. I imagine it's somewhere around three bake sales and a funding drive to combat a single racist headline.

Sometimes, before prayer, I stood in the parking lot of the mosque and watched the cars drive by. I watched them slow down and crank their necks, trying to figure out why two or three police cars were parked outside this place. I watched them come to the realization that it was the mosque that drew all of this hubbub. I watched them and wondered what they must think of us.

∨

Two months after September 11, in November 2001, Fox debuted 24, an action drama starring Kiefer Sutherland as Jack Bauer, an agent with the fictional Counter Terrorist Unit. The show's title was a gimmick: each episode took place over one hour in real time. Split screens showed us what each character was up to in "real time." And a season added up to a full day of terrorist ass-kicking.

The show was not a paragon of high-art television, but it had well-choreographed action, always high-stakes, and a plot twist about every eight minutes. My dad and I fell in love with it quickly. It became a ritual for us: once a week, regardless of the pressures of school or work or life, Baba and I gathered in front of the TV and watched Bauer do his thing.

At first, it was the action that drew us in. Bauer breathed very heavily. Whenever he was charged with a mission, he always said shit like "That's impossible," when it was, in fact, possible. But around the fourth season, our relationship to it changed. The season's main plotline involved a Muslim family—two parents and their son—who were living in America, working as members of an international terrorist cell.

We watched the villains praying like we prayed. We heard words that brought us comfort, words of prayer, coming out of the bad guy's mouth. I remember we laughed, but not the laughter you share at a good joke. It was a laughter of despair. *Is this what they really think of us? Is this how they think we use these words?*

If paranoia was 24's main offering, the justification of torture was a prominent side dish. The show hinged on Jack Bauer's abilities to extract the truth by any means. This included gruesome tactics like hanging his victims from hooks and using sanding machines. In the first five seasons of 24, the Parents Television Council counted sixty-seven torture scenes. That means more than half of the episodes featured a torture set piece.

Years later, Howard Gordon, one of the show's executive producers, was asked if he had any regrets about the ways 24 contributed to a climate of Islamophobia. He named one regret: during the promotion for the fourth season, he noticed that on a prominent highway, a billboard simply read, "They could be next door."

Gordon said the billboard made the producers realize "how dangerous and potentially incendiary this show could be. And I think our awareness of that changed the way we approached the series."

But here's the thing. Gordon gave that interview in the promotional run for the show he created after 24. It was called *Homeland*. The whole premise of *Homeland* is *they could be next door.*

∨

"*Gott ist tot,*" declared Nietzsche. But the man was an atheist, so God wasn't exactly alive to him to begin with. Instead, he meant that Europe's moral centre had shifted. He was watching a radical shift in governance—away from divine right and God as the source of morality, and toward a secular world based on philosophy and science.

Nietzsche wasn't sure that the death of God was going to work out. The change was rather seismic, and he wondered whether Europe could keep hold of its principles without linking them back to God. It's fair to say that Nietzsche would probably hate it if he knew that "God is dead" is now something of a crude shorthand for his challenging body of work.

But if he's upset, he sure can't do anything about it.

In my third year of university, the winning design for the annual Philosophy Department T-shirt featured, in big bold letters on the front, "'GOD IS DEAD'— NIETZSCHE." On the back, in the same big letters, it read, "'NIETZSCHE IS DEAD'—GOD." Get it? It's the kind of joke that is funny to approximately zero per cent of non-philosophy majors.

It's also the kind of joke that's *particularly* unfunny to Muslim dads. Or at least that was the case with Baba. When Baba saw the shirt, he didn't speak a word; he just grabbed it, went to the kitchen, got a pair of scissors, and cut it into ribbons.

I try now to think of what was going through his head. How he'd moved halfway across the world to give his son a chance at a decent life, while worrying all the while that the very same move would threaten the presence of Islam in his son's heart. What it must've felt like to see that son nonchalantly donning a shirt that loudly declared "God is dead."

I try to think of this now because I sure as hell didn't think of it then. At the time, it was just another fracture in the growing rift between me and religion. At home, my waning commitment to prayer had become a source of tension. In pop culture, headlines about Muslims protesting *Harry Potter* collided with talk show hosts telling me that religion was boring and backward.

I read of famous Muslims who had denounced Islam. I listened to them use words I knew, to make the case against Islam. I saw the adoration given to them by a white media landscape that promised to make any Muslim who criticized Islam famous. I saw the positive press coverage they received when they attacked the hijab as regressive and oppressive. They got called "brave" and "freethinkers," and I began to wonder if that's what I wanted, too.

And then I met Dana.

I didn't exactly *mean* to meet Dana. In what should've been my final year of university, I tacked a gender studies class onto my schedule, hoping it would be easy. "Feminism and Islam" was the name of the course, and

I figured I might not know much about feminism but I had a head start on knowing about Islam, so that ought to do the trick.

Dana, the professor for the course, had other ideas. Over twelve weeks, she constructed a meticulous intellectual path that introduced me to ideas like patriarchy, Islamophobia, and orientalism. She rigorously showed a historical thread of racism running through the West's treatment of Muslims, going back centuries. She drilled down into policy decisions like hijab bans and immigration rules, and peeled back the layers of discrimination they're built on. She connected ideas that had never been connected in my mind (*Why do we call them "honour killings" when they're done by Muslims, but call them something else when white men kill their wives?*).

"Feminism and Islam" gave me new language and new tools to dissect the world around me. It introduced me to Arab and Muslim writers who were rejecting the idea that Islam had no room for feminism. These writers—most of them women—had been writing for decades, expanding the definitions of what Islam could be. They'd been critiquing Islam from the inside, without descending to insulting it.

It was thrilling and intimidating. A crash course in ideas that had touched my life deeply, even though I didn't know it. I began to realize that I didn't know Islam at all. Perhaps I didn't know the world I was living in at all. It dawned on me that my philosophy education, with its fancy focus on metaphysics and Kantian ethics, wasn't going to be of much help.

I could've graduated at the end of that term. I had enough credits. But halfway through the semester, I formally changed my major to gender studies. I knew this meant I'd have to stay an extra year at university. I also knew that this was the only way for my education to have value.

❮

The first time I received hate mail, it was in a generously assembled package. I could tell that a great amount of care went into it.

It arrived three weeks after I appeared on a TV panel. A thick envelope addressed to me, delivered to the BuzzFeed offices. Inside it, carefully folded, were printouts of two tweets where I mentioned I'm a Muslim—something I rarely tweet about—in addition to several other printouts of tweets by some prominent bigots and Islamophobes, photos of women in niqabs, and a note about why I should've learned that Western values are superior by now.

The note ended with a question, carefully high-lighted in yellow:

If you have to pick one, which?

1. Promote and teach superior values to immigrants.
2. Accept and be tolerant of inferior values of immigrants.

The letter didn't come with a sender's name, but there was a PO Box address attached. For a brief moment, I considered writing back. But what would I even say? Maybe something like:

Dear Sir/Madam,

I don't fucking need this. I'm struggling with how Muslim I am in this land in the first place. You see, you read the tweets and you see my name and you automatically assume that I am applying myself to my faith. Let me assure you that, if I was doing so, I would not be bothering with a response. Instead, I identify as a languishing Muslim, one who sorely misses the way Islam imposed itself on the social order in the land I once called home.

Because that meant I didn't have a choice. Here, it's easier to become lethargic and half-heartedly Muslim. It's easier to let doubt about faith become the default state. And when there's even a little bit of doubt, it's hard to do the work. See, Islam is actually a lot of work. I mean, five prayers a day! Funny story about that: the Qur'an says that, originally, Allah told the Prophet that there should be fifty prayers a day. However, thanks to a rigorous negotiation process, it went down to five. But back to your question . . .

As it turns out, this was my introduction to Islamophobic mail, a reality I've lived with since then. On occasion, I receive emails about my name ("your name scares me lol"), my beard ("your beard is shit"), and just about anything else under the sun ("I would like to see you wearing white robe with long beard walking for hours trying to find a white girl to tell her to dress up"). They all add up to the same thing: as a TV Muslim, I have become, in the eyes of some viewers, the avatar of what's wrong with Islam.

The most intense iteration of this came when a Canadian right-wing YouTuber made a video arguing that Islam is slowly taking over Canadian media. In it, she spliced together several of my TV appearances discussing Islamophobia in the news, and used me as her incontrovertible evidence of The Takeover™.

Over forty minutes (seriously), like a sports anchor, the YouTuber performed a play-by-play analysis ("He's trying to say he wants the practices of his tribe to be accepted, without saying it") to guide viewers to the conclusion that I am intent on bending the narrative to pacify Canadian media in preparation for Muslims to introduce sharia law.

The YouTube video was a thorough document. Its host had gone to extraordinary lengths to dissect my words sentence by sentence to land the argument that I am a Muslim sleeper agent. What bothered me most about this is that *I* felt like a hypocrite—if I was going to be cast as a sleeper agent anyway, perhaps I shouldn't be so lazy about faith. Perhaps I should put the work in to be a more convincing sleeper agent.

I learned that suspicion could come in the form of a careless look, or the form of someone who cares a lot to let you know how suspicious they are.

∨

As is custom with every Liverpool player, Salah gets his own chant. Fans changed the lyrics to the top UK hit "Sit

Down" by Manchester band James to sing his praises. The original lyrics, "Oh, sit down! Oh, sit down! Sit down next to me," became "Mo Salah! Mo Salah! Running down the wing!" It's a simple sentiment set to a classic tune, and it spread like wildfire among the fans. You can hear it sung in every Liverpool fan bar around the world.

After Salah's heroics in his first season at Liverpool—his goals in the quarterfinals and semifinals of the Champions League helped the club get to the final—a new chant was born. It goes, "If he's good enough for you, he's good enough for me / If he scores another few then I'll be Muslim too."

Scores of white fans shout this when Salah steps onto the pitch. They shout it at the top of their lungs, and it fills me with wonder. Do they know what they're saying? They'll be Muslim too? Britain saw a marked increase in hate crimes against Muslims between 2015 and 2020, and here they are singing about how they're this close to being Muslim?

"If he's good enough for you, he's good enough for me / Then sitting in a mosque is where I want to be." But when the fans sing this song, I know they do not actually mean they want to sit closer in proximity to the danger, the terror, that comes with being Muslims in a land that fears them.

❯

I cannot predict what my daughter's relationship to Islam will be. I cannot say if the tether will be as strong as mine. After Amna was born, the first melody to grace her ears was the adhan. She'd been in the world for less than an hour when Baba gently sang it into her right ear. It is not a repeating motif for her the same way it was for me, but it is my job to make sure it is not a distant and foreign melody.

In many ways, we're a long way from 24. We're a long way from *Homeland*. Shows like *NCIS: Los Angeles* and *Blindspot* prominently feature Muslim characters. Riz Ahmed can front Oscar-nominated films, and Rami Malek can win a lead actor Oscar. It is not the same post-9/11 media representation for Muslims and Arabs I grew up with.

A Stanford study found that, since Salah joined Liverpool, hate crimes in the city have dropped by 19 per cent. In the same period, hate crimes went up in the rest of Britain, and a fraught Brexit process didn't help. It's impossible to pin Liverpool's drop on Salah alone, but his presence can't be ignored, either.

For so many Muslims, so many Arabs, day-to-day life hasn't changed much. The racism and discrimination and suspicious looks are still a common enough experience. But a North Star has appeared. We can watch one of ours be one of the best in the world at something, and ride on his coattails.

There are Arab and Muslim children who don't know a world without Salah's influence. They don't know what it's like to see yourself *only* represented as a terrorist on TV. They hear songs about people who aren't us, who want to be a little like us—and for them, this is normal.

I can't help but be envious of that, because I was born Muslim and then the world made that identity a site of conflict for me. I can't help but relish the freedom they have to imagine themselves as something more— to allow their religion to be one of many identities they can inhabit. That freedom becomes a defence in the face of all-too-present Islamophobia.

It's a hard-won freedom I never thought possible. Like when you're caged in by bodies. Closed in by formations intent on shutting you down, and you feel the space getting tighter.

But Salah spins and pivots and the bodies disappear. He turns and slides and the formations crumble. And he takes off running, running, running, because he knows what's behind him. And he shoots like he's always known where the goalposts are. He doesn't have to look. He just knows.

SEVEN

The Metal Kids

Grinning from ear to ear, I pushed my way through the pool of exuberant bodies and collective sweat and emerged on the other side victorious. My body was pulsating with the vibrating bass, ears ringing from the symphony of distorted guitars. My shirt clung to me with desperation from all the sweat and beer that had been spilled. I was dehydrated and aching, with a small cut on the left side of my face. And it was the happiest moment of my life.

I made my way to Mama, who was standing politely on the side, doing her best to hide a look of horror. She adjusted her hijab as, all around her, well-mohawked and aggressively pierced and heavily eyelinered people stood to take a breather. She offered me water and a cookie. I took the water, but wanted to appear hardcore so I turned down the cookie.

"Your face!" she exclaimed over the music. I lifted my hand to my forehead and felt around for the war wound. I looked at my finger, bearing a familiar crimson. I knew that crowd surfer had got me good, but I didn't know he'd got me *this* good.

"And why do they do this?" Mama asked me.

"What do you mean *this*?" I asked with joy. She gestured behind me at the mass of bodies thrashing, crashing into itself, like an unrelenting sea. I thought about the answer for a moment, trying to express it in Arabic, but I didn't think I could do it justice. What's Arabic for "mosh pit"? What's Arabic for "I know it looks like disorder, but a good mosh pit will keep you safe and protect you"? In there, the music is always two notches louder than your anger. The wall of sound will subsume your pain, amplify it. It's a safe place for unsafe emotions. You won't emerge healed, but you might emerge, for a moment, redeemed.

But David Draiman was finishing his rant and the chords of "Rise" were beginning to ring through the hall. The song was from Disturbed's recently released second album, and you could tell excitement was building in the pit by the way bodies were beginning to once again pick up speed, like molecules exposed to a fire. I couldn't miss this.

I smiled at Mama, shouted "Gotta go!" and grabbed the cookie. As I headed back toward the mosh pit, I spotted the crowd-surfing kid who not long ago drew blood. He pointed at my hand and said, "Is that a fucking cookie in the mosh pit?" I hesitantly nodded. He shot back, "That's fucking tight. Let's go!"

I gave Mama a quick wave, turned around, and vanished again into this chaotic sea of mercy.

˅

Everything was a fight. *Everything* was a fight.

Mama and Baba had seemingly underestimated the potential conflicts that could come from moving their teenage son to Canada. Once we arrived, my parents wanted to delicately balance acknowledging that we existed in Canada and limiting my exposure to actual Canadians. They knew I'd be spending all day at school with people who didn't necessarily share the same values, and they wanted to protect and preserve my Islamic and Sudanese identity for as long as possible. Their go-to method for this was applying a blanket "no" to any of my attempts to branch out beyond the house.

Can I hang out at a new friend's house? No. Can I go to a sleepover? Nopity nope. A school dance? Nuh-uh. Can I go out after school? Yes: to the library to meet the English tutor, and then straight home. Can I go out on the weekend? No, you have to help Baba with the store.

My new friends grew familiar with my restrictions, which included but were not limited to: can't hang after school, can't go to the mall during lunch, can't meet at the movie theatre for the 8 p.m. showing of *28 Days Later*. On the rare occasion I was permitted to go over to a friend's house—well, I better be home by seven. Seven!!!!!!

My early teen years were more defined by what I couldn't do than what I could do. And as a young immigrant, this meant all the effort I invested in making new friends was undone by my inability to spend time with them outside of a school setting. I was left with FOMO and resentment.

Walking home from school was always the hardest. We left school together, joyous and rambunctious, and then when we made it past the grocery store I abruptly had to break off from the pack, homebound. Cutting through the alley behind an apartment complex, I could hear the laughter and jokes continue on merrily. Without me.

The one thing that wasn't a problem for my parents was helping Baba with the store. My parents didn't mind me spending my evenings there, as long as I used the time to do homework and occasionally worked the cash. But hey—it beat staring at the wall at home, so I took what I could get.

Working at the store became a symbol of my entrapment. I could think of a million places I would rather be, and yet here I was—either doing homework, or standing across from a customer who planned to spend $500 in break-open lottery tickets but would only do so $10 at a time. At the end of the day, I also had the boring job of killing time waiting for Baba to finish paperwork.

I often stood at the corner of the counter, pretending to dust, or took care of recycling the day's newspapers. But what I was actually doing was trying desperately to stand on my tippy-toes to catch a glimpse of the covers of the sealed porn magazines. An attempt to push back against the boundaries placed on me.

It was in the middle of this over-policing that I met Will.

Will was a tall, big dude who worked the night shift at the store. The first time I met him, I remember thinking he was unlike anyone I'd ever met. He had an eyebrow piercing, something I'd never seen on a man.

He was bald and bearded, and physically looked like he could beat you up, but his cherub face betrayed that he could never actually do it.

Mostly, Will kept to himself. The night shift meant he didn't have to deal with a lot of people: he had to restock the shelves, clean the store, and take out the garbage. To keep himself company, he brought a giant boom box and a massive collection of CDs.

Will's shift started at eleven. He had a little ritual: he'd arrive fifteen minutes early and set up his boom box behind the counter. He'd rifle through his CDs and pick one to put on at a low volume while Baba was still in the front. Then, when Baba went to the back office, he'd switch CDs and turn up the volume while handling the first round of cleaning, belting out songs.

Observing Will being free and uninhibited, shouting lyrics I didn't understand with piercings I didn't understand, was intriguing. I began to spend more time with him while Baba did his work. Most of it was just spent noticing how utterly different we were: me, beholden, limited; him, so entirely himself.

One day, after an argument with Baba, I was sulking in the corner when Will came in and set up his music. As Baba disappeared into the back, I heard the words from the boom box, a hoarse screaming voice paired with chunky, driving, heavy guitars and resonant drums: "Shout! Shout! Let it all out! These are the things I can do without!"

Will turned it up and walked away, singing to himself. I was engrossed and captivated; I'd never met rage in music before. Sudanese music was about love and longing. Music that vacillated between joy and heartbreak, but did so with a focus on clarity and exaggerated poetic beauty. Sonically, clean electric guitars and brass instruments reigned. But there was nothing beautiful or clean about what I was hearing now; it was a chaotic cacophony of distortion. Whoever was singing sounded *pissed*. I didn't pick up all the words, but I was lost in the tone. I felt inside what this man was expressing out loud.

When Will returned, I begged to know who this was and what they were so angry about. "That's Disturbed," he told me.

"Disturbed? And what does *disturbed* mean."

"Ha! Hmmm, how do I explain *disturbed*? It's like . . . upset or a little crazy."

The notion that a band would name themselves after being in a state of distress was astonishing to me. The music I grew up with extended as far as protest and rebellion. But imbalance? Never. So a band building their identity around being crazy and sounding angry and explicitly not beautiful was something entirely beyond the ethos of what music was to me. It sounded urgent and explosive and impolite. It didn't ask for your attention; it just took it.

I asked Will to play me another song. He played "Voices," which sounded haunted and unhinged. The delivery of the singing was frantic and the guitars were agitated. "Play me another," I said, anxious but captivated. Thick drums filled the room, building up to a guttural scream and a driving chord progression as powerful as they were scary.

The first time you hear "Down with the Sickness," it can unsettle you. "I can see inside you, the sickness is rising / Don't try to deny what you feel," posits David Draiman. The song is an invitation to feel unsavoury emotions you've been suppressing ("Open up your hate and let it flow into me"). It culminates in a gruesome spoken bridge that describes a child screaming while being physically beaten by his mother, before he retaliates by killing her. It's a lot for anyone to hear. But it's especially shocking to someone who thought all music was about love or the flowers that bloom beside the Nile.

I noticed that my fists were clenched while listening to *The Sickness*, and that I felt better afterwards, as though someone had untied a knot in my core. And it made sense. After spending a day trying not to think about feeling imprisoned in the store, the overwhelming fury of the sound reached out from the stereo, saw me, and amalgamated my anger. It felt like a moment of radical honesty—Disturbed welcomed my frustrations, made room for them. The music itself was the resolution: if you lived in the song, it could house you until the storm of emotion passed.

I borrowed the CD from Will, went home, and stayed up listening to *The Sickness* over and over again until I fell asleep.

v

The explosion of nu metal was a brief and blinding supernova event, confined to a short window at the turn of the century. It was a blip in music history, and is widely considered now to be an embarrassing one.

You can hear the germ of the sound in Korn's first two albums, or Deftones' *Adrenaline* or Sepultura's *Roots*. But then it exploded in popularity after it was commercially framed as an answer to the mega-pop sound of the nineties. Think Backstreet Boys and Ace of Base.

The history of rock looks unkindly upon the era of nu metal, in part because the abrasive noise was misunderstood as little but combustible rage. Unlike the logical political anger found at the birth of punk, or the rebellion in musical aesthetics that gave us heavy metal, nu metal's essence and raison d'être were seen as anger for anger's sake. Its content was apparently the warmed leftovers of Gen X's directionlessness, which had birthed the grunge scene ("The captain is drunk, your world is Titanic," Limp Bizkit complained).

The sound was, on purpose, chaotic and unvarnished. The music was loud and occasionally unpleasant. The guitars were almost universally in drop D tuning, so the low notes could reach even lower. Power chords were ascendant. The voices were hoarse and strained and occasionally unintelligible—nu metal was marked with growling and grunting and quick-paced syncopated scream-singing. The lyrics were anti-authority and obsessed with nihilism, because of course they were.

At the turn of the century, the children of baby boomers were becoming teenagers, a decade after Foster Cline and Jim Fay coined the term *helicopter parent*. These millennials were exhausted from being watched too closely, dissatisfied with the weight of expectations, and often living in subdivisions cut off from the vitality of the city. In these new neighbour-hoods, the houses looked alike and existed in a protected bubble, away from the urban life force. At the same time, anxiety about the overmedication of teens grew. Lonely and separated and lost, for these teens the empty parking lot of the strip mall was their church because there was nothing interesting for miles.

Nu metal felt like a pipeline of raw, unrefined anger, delivered to the kids who needed it. At the time, there were no significant pop-culture articulations of the small wounds of suburbia: boredom, pointlessness, and an overwhelming loss of agency. It's no wonder that nu metal has often been described as music for teenagers whose parents wouldn't let them have the family car on a Friday night. In *Spin* magazine, Charles Aaron called it "slam-dancing-in-a-high-chair" music.

Critics may have whinged and protested, but none of that mattered because the audience was eating up the music. Korn's 1998 album, *Follow the Leader*, which gave us the gruff scaffolding and vocal textures that became the signature of nu metal—proved this music could sell. The album went five-times platinum.

Alongside Korn, the other pioneers were bands like Limp Bizkit, Godsmack and Staind. The late 1990s witnessed a gold rush in this new sound: Sevendust, Papa Roach, Seether, Saliva, Alien Ant Farm, Crazy Town, Trapt, Chevelle, Shinedown, Unloco, Taproot—I could go on.

None of this went over well with the metal community at large—a community that was witnessing the art it had developed turned into formulaic commercial angst. Limp Bizkit released a much-maligned (or for some of us, celebrated) cover of George Michael's "Faith." Slipknot signed a colossal seven-album deal. *Rock Hard* magazine published a cover with a tombstone, declaring the death of heavy metal.

By 2000, nu metal was a verifiable force on the radio, MTV was playing Limp Bizkit as often as they did Britney Spears, and Hot Topic sold Slipknot T-shirts in every mall. And a band from a small suburb outside Los Angeles managed to distill the raw energy of the angst in the air, refine it, and pour it all into twelve songs. Their debut album, *Hybrid Theory*, had a softer touch than Limp Bizkit or Korn, and this soft touch changed everything. It took the escalating popularity of nu metal into the stratosphere.

The first time I heard Linkin Park was also through Will. After giving back the Disturbed CD, I begged for more bands like this; I needed heavy sounds and anger. He nonchalantly picked out *Hybrid Theory* and handed it to me.

I put it in my Discman while Dad busied himself with work. The impact was immediate—a jolt of recognition at the straightforward lyrics and the music that mirrored my internal chaos. "I cannot take this anymore," Chester Bennington sung, and it was electrifying to hear exactly how I felt spelled out in a song.

Linkin Park were often criticized for simple lyrics and metaphors. But those criticisms overlook that the simplicity *is the point.* "Everything you say to me / Takes me one step closer to the edge / And I'm about to break," sings Bennington, and there is nothing ambiguous about what he means: he is giving voice to the listener. And in the store that day, he was giving voice to my inner dialogue.

At that time, I fantasized about blowout arguments I would have with my parents. And Linkin Park provided a soundtrack to these frustrations. I wasn't brave enough to push back, but here was this man crossing the line I dreamed of crossing. "Shut up when I'm talking to you," he screamed, and I felt at peace.

This music made me feel understood, and it had never occurred to me that this was something music could *do.* And it wasn't just about resolving conflict with my parents. On days when I felt self-conscious about having an accent, I could go home and bury myself in Bennington bellowing "I felt this way before / So insecure."

After buying my own copy of the album, I walked around school listening to it over and over. My favourite song on it, "Runaway," felt like it was written just for me. It describes an atmosphere of "A constant wave of tension / On top of broken trust," and crescendos into a chorus of "I wanna run away / Never say goodbye." In short: *same*.

❯

Listening to *Hybrid Theory* and *The Sickness* meant I had an in with the metal kids. They were the ones standing in the margins, where they had each other and music that understood them. They felt trapped by the suburbs and I felt trapped by my parents, and maybe we didn't have a lot in common but we could sit together in that trapped feeling—and having that company was everything.

Linkin Park became the foundation for my first deep high school friendships. And it all started with Aaron.

Aaron moved between social groups, but mostly he hung around with the Christian kids. We'd known each other for a couple of years, but didn't really talk much until we discovered a mutual love of Linkin Park.

Aaron was outgoing and generous—he went out of

his way to make people feel welcome—and I was in awe of the ease with which he made people laugh. His easygoing nature made him the guy everyone shared their problems with. He always responded with empathy and patience and good advice.

The fact that he was Christian made it easier for us to relate to each other. In a time when it seemed like everyone in high school was smoking weed or drinking, my way of clinging to Islam was to avoid those things. I felt sure that drinking and smoking weren't for me, but I resented that abstaining made me stand out. For Aaron, the certainty came easily—he could playfully deflect a joint or turn down a drink without losing people's attention. So I began hanging around his group of friends, and watched the ways he worked his magic. I wanted to have that sparkle.

Aaron was the youngest of four boys. He was navigating a busy household and dealing with the pressure of a new relationship, and I knew that he, like me, processed his anxiety through music. We talked about how we'd blast the stereo and turn off the lights and lie face down on the floor to let Linkin Park flow through us when we needed it. Talking to him made me feel recognized.

When the *Hybrid Theory* follow-up *Meteora* dropped in 2003, we hurried to school the next day to talk about it. The album connected with even more electricity than its predecessor had. For Aaron, the album spoke directly to stormy tensions at home, and the enormous burden of being everyone's problem solver. For me, it mapped perfectly onto the inexpressible pains of adolescence I was dealing with. There was "Somewhere I Belong" ("I wanna heal, I wanna feel like I'm close to something real"). There was "Breaking the Habit" ("I don't know what's worth fighting for / Or why I have to scream").

But the song that landed the hardest for me was "Numb," which I immediately adopted as a new anthem—the song I word-for-word needed to say to Mama and Baba ("Can't you see that you're smothering me / Holding too tightly, afraid to lose control / 'Cause everything that you thought I would be / Has fallen apart right in front of you"). It was a clearer articulation of the strain between me and my parents than I was capable of.

Meteora became the connective tissue that bonded me to Aaron. We understood that, though the ways the world impacted each of us were unique, the feelings of hurt, anger, and containment were shared. And so too were the antidotes, because we knew that there was nothing a primal scream and a distorted guitar couldn't drown out, just for a moment.

Through Aaron, I met a cadre of church kids who felt safe. We had a lot in common—the slightly religious background, the skepticism of drugs, the difficulty of family expectations. And we could all see ourselves in Linkin Park.

Sean was a fashionable, puka-necklaced kid with too much hair gel and a big laugh. Luke was lanky and quiet. Unsurprisingly, the news that these guys were the people I wanted to spend time with made my parents relax their rules a little. I could now come home at, say, nine! They felt they could trust the Christian kids because at least we had an Abrahamic god in common, or something.

When Aaron got his driver's licence, a group of us piled into his parents' van and drove around the neighbourhood, blasting the album. We drove to the conservation area and left the car stereo blaring as we played soccer in the field. We told each other secrets and whispered the names of the girls we were in love with that week. We played video games we won't remember the names of, holding on only to the memories of laughter and closeness and the comfort that comes with needing a person who needs you—and Linkin Park was the soundtrack to all of it.

We understood that when Chester Bennington roared, he was fending off our demons so that we could breathe easy.

∨

When Disturbed announced they would be touring to support their second album, I held my breath. The Music as a Weapon II tour—a nod to their song "Droppin' Plates," where Draiman vows to "fight the war / And use my music as a weapon"—would almost certainly stop in Toronto.

I developed a little plan. After dutifully doing *every* chore for two weeks and avoiding all conflict with Mama and Baba, I would approach my parents and ask them if *please, pretty please*, I could go see this band that had transformed me. I knew Baba trusted Will, so I planned to ask if Will could take me to the concert. I'd pay for it out of my own money from working at the store.

The plan mostly went off without a hitch. Except for one addendum, a tiny little change: I could go, but . . . Mama had to come, too.

What? Internally, I fell apart. *I'm fifteen! I don't want to take my mom to a concert! What the hell would she do at a metal concert anyway?* Externally, I kept my cool: if it meant I got to see the band of my dreams, then yeah, I *guessed* this was fine.

We arrived at the venue early. Like, *way* early. Doors at 7 p.m., show at eight? We got there at three. We weren't the only early ones—I recognized my fellow outcasts, dressed in all black, sitting on the sidewalk with nothing to do but wait for the show. It was a desolate area of town, all warehouses and factories, so no one had anywhere to go. Will and Mama and I walked to the street behind the venue, in search of a place to sit and grab a meal, but with no luck. There was nothing nearby. And then . . . I heard a familiar bassline reverberating, bouncing off the handful of buildings on the side street. "Do you hear that?!" I said with exhilaration. "It's the bass part of 'Intoxication'!"

Before Will or Mama could respond, I took off running, chasing after the sound. I found the source: a small door was propped open with a garbage can, and through the opening the notes came wafting out. Without thinking, I slipped through the door and moved the black curtain that stood behind it out of the way. And there they were.

Onstage, bassist Steve "Fuzz" Kmak and guitarist Dan Donegan stood face to face, their guitars forming a perfect X, their bodies bobbing in unison as they played. Behind them, seated amidst a comically large drum set, Mike Wengren banged his way through the song I recognized. My heart was beating out of my chest. Offstage and to the side, vocalist David Draiman stood, signing autographs for a handful of fans wearing badges around their necks.

I had accidentally stumbled upon Disturbed's soundcheck. Aside from the band and the crew, it was just me and a half-dozen fans who'd won a contest to attend. The reality set in that I was in an empty hall before my idols, and I completely froze. Stagehands and tour technicians whizzed past me, each with a job to do, while I was a statue of awe, my jaw wide open.

Draiman began to approach me, perhaps thinking I was among the contest winners here to witness the soundcheck. *Oh fuck, is he going to talk to me?* A complete panic took over my whole body. I turned around and ran as fast as I could toward the door.

I emerged back on the street to a scornful look from Mama and a "what the fuck are you doing?" glance from Will. He knew how hard I'd had to work to convince my parents to let me come, so the recklessness of my running away and disappearing into a forbidden zone was probably confusing.

But I didn't care. For the whole episode, which probably lasted six minutes, I had felt something I longed for: to be free to get into trouble; to sneak into back doors and smuggle myself into soundchecks; to risk something to see a band I loved. I felt unshackled, like all of the negotiations I'd had to go through with my parents were inconsequential. I was throbbing with joy.

In line to get into the venue, I overheard a group discussing what they anticipated would be on the set list, and I burst out with the news that I'd accidentally snuck into the soundcheck earlier and they were playing "Intoxication." Their reaction was exactly the validation I needed—they looked at me like I was a hero, and asked me to detail my adventure. And I did, as though I was Moses telling tales of the mountain.

What had made me feel judged and aware of my limitations just minutes before had transformed into a reason to be celebrated. I wrapped myself in this feeling as long as I could. These were my people. I didn't tell them Mama had cookies in her purse for me.

∨

The nu metal moment was over as fast as it began, in part because the scene couldn't sustain so many copycats. We didn't know it that day at the Disturbed concert, but 2003 would be the beginning of the end.

The bands began to sell less, so they started retreating from the sound. Kid Rock's country single "Picture" sold better than the nu metal–sounding songs off his *Cocky* album. Bands like Drowning Pool and Papa Roach abandoned the throaty, groovy hallmarks of the sound in favour of a straightforward hard rock style. Meanwhile,

Staind's Aaron Lewis became a dad and released a ballad about his daughter called "Zoe Jane." It's a lovely, optimistic song about fatherhood that only contains approximately 3 per cent angst.

The nail in the coffin came in 2007, when Linkin Park released *Minutes to Midnight*, an album that traded the nu metal sound for complex melodies and downright *beautiful* singing. It was still angry and sad, but it was polished in its sorrow. The genre's biggest draw made a graceful exit, and it gave permission for the rest of us to leave the moment behind, too.

Unlike other genres that go through ebbs and flows, revivals and recessions, nu metal stayed dead. In 2012, Limp Bizkit frontman Fred Durst put it this way: "Say in 2000, there were 35 million people who connected to this band . . . lots of those people have moved on. We were a moment in time and it's over."

Durst was right. The over-the-top rage and overbearing guitars that had served the suburban kids in 1999 were out of place even by 2003, when there were actual horrors to be mad about: the War on Terror and the Iraq War, for starters. The obsession with personal pain seemed so out-of-place and self-indulgent, and the genre never recovered. In 2017, Incubus vocalist Brandon Boyd told *The Guardian*, "When I hear that term [nu metal], it makes my palms sweat . . . it always made me cringe."

In 2014, I met up with Aaron and a handful of high school friends to see Linkin Park. All of us were married, grown men by then, so distant from the twelve-year-olds we were when we fell in love with the band, when they knew how to translate our pain better than we did. They played more than two dozen songs that night, an act of generosity for those in attendance who wanted to revisit those past selves, those fragile children, to tell them everything was okay now.

As the familiar walloping guitars of "Faint" ascended from the stage and exploded off the walls of the arena, I saw myself in the thousands around me, their eyes lit up with a recognition of the feeling that moved through their bodies. We glowed in the light of the music that had once punched through speakers and formed a shield around us, protecting us from the darkness.

We stood from our seats in the nosebleed section, and instinctively wrapped our arms around each other, thrashing wildly, in the way you can only manage if you feel held.

EIGHT

Roads (Part III)

Mama's heart is weak, in the professional opinion of medical experts and their advanced medical devices. They say it's getting tired of pumping blood to the rest of her body. But with all due respect, they don't know Mama's heart like I do.

Mama lost her mother when she was ten, and her father when she was fifteen. She was raised by her half-sister, Mama Reja, who was a second mother to me growing up. Reja was a mountain of strength for Mama.

When Mama graduated high school, she worked for Sudan's Ministry of Finance before she got married at twenty-six. Three years later, I came along. And two years after that, Baba left Sudan searching for a better life in Kuwait.

The plan was: he'd go, get himself established, then Mama and I would join him. Saddam Hussein, however, had other ideas—namely, invading Kuwait and kicking off a war. Now Baba needed to figure out a way to escape Kuwait, but there were no flights out of the country. He left just days before the carnage, fleeing in a car with relatives. The plan was to cross into Iraq and fly out of Baghdad. As they drove toward the border, they held their breath as Iraqi forces sped in the opposite direction, on their way to wreak havoc.

Mama didn't think Baba was going to make it. She thought he was going to die in Kuwait, brutalized like the thousands of civilians who lost their lives in the Gulf War. She began imagining what life would be like as the widowed mother of a two-year-old. Where was she going to live? Would she need to go back to work?

Baba came home safely, but it's not like Sudan was an oasis. The regime of Omar al-Bashir was engaged in an active campaign to crack down on political dissent. Government forces harassed us. They rounded up my mom's older brother, Mustafa, and threw him in jail for his involvement with the opposition.

My parents came to the realization that this was not the environment they wanted to raise their only son in. So, in February 1995, a few months before my parents' tenth wedding anniversary—and a month before my seventh birthday—Baba packed his bags again, this time Switzerland-bound.

For five long years after that, Mama had to be both Mama and Baba. She had to contend with a young boy who was just learning how far he could push his tired mother. Then, after all that, at forty-one, she left behind all of her family and all of her friends and went to a land where she knew few people and didn't speak the language.

She'd endured unimaginable heartbreak and pain at such an early age. Strife followed her, and fear for the people she loved coloured her life. She played the parts of both parents for years. And then she transplanted herself to another world. I saw how her tolerance for struggle surpassed all reasonable limits.

So, with respect to the heart doctors, they don't know Mama's heart like I do.

❤

I began cultivating a hope, and I should've known better. I wanted, more than anything, to go to Carleton University in Ottawa. Its red-brick buildings looked amazing in the brochures, okay? I'm very shallow. But more than the red brick, it was a full 196 kilometres away from my parents—a safe distance at which to spread my wings.

I fantasized about the day we would all pile into the van and hit the 401 eastbound. I wanted the moment you see in the movies: a big hug from Mama and Baba, then watching them drive away after moving me into a dorm. I longed for the split second I turned around and saw a campus that belonged to me.

So I planned the sell. I talked it up to Baba. Since the agreement was for me to go to law school eventually, and Carleton was one of very few universities to offer an undergraduate law program, I said I'd go there and be among the most prepared applicants to law school in four years. An undergrad in law *before* law school? Damn, no one would be more ready than me! Look at me, a young lawyer in the making.

I anticipated the counterarguments, too. Too expensive? Well, I'm taking a student loan either way—what's an extra li'l bit. Too far? The Greyhound could have me home in two hours, the train even faster. I planned to name-drop the Sudanese families in Ottawa. *I could even make more Sudanese friends, isn't that what you want?*

This was a non-starter. As far as Baba saw it, I had to go to Queen's, and I had to live at home. Baba's counter-arguments: Queen's had a better reputation, and I would graduate with a significantly smaller debt. "We don't have the kind of money the white kids have," he told me. Plus, if I stayed at home, I could keep my part-time hours as a cashier, he said.

Mama backed him up on this. "I know the Canadians leave home," she said, "but we didn't sacrifice and come from Sudan for you to leave us. You'll live at home."

I was wounded, feeling caged. I listened to what they had to say, but all I took from it was: *No, you can't leave home. You'll do what we tell you to do.*

❧

If you're travelling east to Kingston and you have to make a stop—trust me, you want to take the Port Hope rest stop. Yes, it feels a little soon, coming only fifty kilometres after you clear the Ajax traffic bottleneck. But if you think you can get what you need later, that's wishful thinking.

The next rest stop is Trenton, and it's a logical midway point on your journey—except it is undeniably the worst rest stop. The food selection is limited, the parking is awkward, and no one is ever happy to see you there. Take your pee break at Port Hope, and enjoy the modern amenities, the clean bathrooms, and the superior choices for food.

Take the early exit. Give yourself this one luxury. Sometimes we miss the good things we deserve because we think they'll magically be given to us later.

❯

On a hot day in the summer of 2006, the morning of the Edgefest music festival, I was sweating with nerves. The whole spring, I'd been talking to Emily, a magnetic woman I met at the end of my first year at university. After exams ended, she returned to her hometown, and I was left constantly thinking about her—the way she threw her head back when she laughed, the intimate softness of her voice. Talking to Emily felt like *this conversation is our treasured secret, and nothing else exists outside of it.*

While she was 330 kilometres west, down the 401, we spoke on the phone, for hours at a time. But I was too chickenshit to tell her how I felt, how I thought about her all the time. And unfortunately for me, her radar for my flirting was, uh, let's say . . . in need of calibration. All my compliments flew right past her.

So I couldn't directly tell her how much I was into her, she couldn't pick up on my vibes, and I couldn't do anything about it. Great. What *could* I do? Well, this is where the radio stepped in. I won tickets to Edgefest, an all-day music festival in Toronto being held on Canada Day. *Perfect*, I thought. *It's right between her hometown and me. I'll just invite her to the show!* Except, if you recall from the previous paragraph, I was profoundly chicken-shit. I invited her as a part of a large group of friends so as to avoid even the *slightest* hint of my intentions.

And so, when I boarded the bus on the way to Edgefest, I was sweating with nerves. Nerves the highway couldn't calm. Like, *yes! I'm about to see the woman who has been occupying my thoughts for months!* But also . . . *no!! I'm about to see the woman who has been occupying my thoughts for months!!*

I spent the entire concert—and remember, this is an all-day music festival—trying to get a quiet moment beside Emily, to give a strong hint that I was into her. We bonded over the music, particularly over a gripping performance from Keane (a band now most famous for being a Coldplay Lite) who were in fine form that day. I inched closer—or at least imagined I was inching closer—to telling her. But every chance I got, I began to stammer and abandoned the mission. My clearest shot came as we were all dawdling out of the venue, and for a split second, we were walking beside each other. The moment couldn't have been more perfect. Above us, Canada Day fireworks lit up the sky and cast a soft glow on our faces. I inhaled and decided this was the time to say something. And then . . .

I felt a friend's hands on my shoulders and, before I could turn around, that friend had climbed on my back and was shouting "ONWARD! PIGGYBACK RIDE!!!!!!!"

Fuck.

❤

The 401 upended the hierarchy of Ontario's economy. For decades, the province's economic engines had been built around water and steel. Goods primarily moved either along the St. Lawrence River and the Great Lakes or by rail, so cities naturally centralized around ports and train stations. Entire ancillary industries organized themselves near these hubs. That's where you'd find banks, restaurants, shops—all the things that make up what we know of city life. But the introduction of the 401 accelerated a shift already underway, replacing boats and trains with cars and trucks.

For ports, this was devastating. Toronto's downtown became derelict and rundown. Beautiful old buildings along the waterfront were turned into parking lots, or were simply left vacant and forgotten. It stayed that way for decades—the area didn't start to recover until the late 1980s and early 1990s.

Established, familiar highways suffered in the shadow of the 401, too. Take Ontario's Highway 2, for example. The road was once the main east–west artery of Southern Ontario. It dates back to the late 1700s and was so central to Ontario's development that, by 1917, it was designated "The Provincial Highway." But most of its route was bypassed by the 401, a wider highway with a faster speed limit. By 1998, Highway 2 lost its highway designation. It was "downloaded," in transportation policy parlance—meaning the responsibility of its maintenance was taken off the province's hands and handed to the myriad municipalities along its route who could barely care for it.

It's a funny thing to decommission a highway. It's not like you can erase the well-worn route from existence. The path of Highway 2 is still driveable—a slower, bumpier ride than the 401. The towns it passes through, once lively waystations for travellers along a key highway, have come to be known by that stinging pejorative, "bedroom communities"—insignificant limbs of the burgeoning metropolis. Highway 2 is a quieter, more meditative drive. But if you pay attention, you'll find its shoulder teeming with the ghosts of its past vibrancy.

The new highway pulled focus. It became the province's lifeblood. It opened up new worlds, forged new possibilities. But the old worlds never ceased to exist. They just stayed there, unwatered, wilting just out of frame.

v

"Okay, well . . . I'm wondering if, when you come back to Kingston, you'd go on a date with me."

I blurted this out on the phone to Emily. I didn't *plan* to, per se, but I'd been wanting to say it for a whole month after the failure to launch at the music festival. And now it was out there. I was relieved the words had finally escaped my mouth, but the relief was quickly replaced by panic after she took what felt like an eternity to respond with an "uh . . ." I felt sure it was going to be followed by ". . . thank you?"—that it was Alice all over again.

"Sure?" she said.

Excellent. Just the kind of buy-in I was hoping for. A yes-questionmark.

I waited an extra six weeks after she came back to Kingston to actually make the date happen. I thought about the ease with which we talked on the phone. The freedom to be myself that came with it. In front of all my friends, I'd long been the loud, boisterous one. But not with Emily. Talking to her naturally allowed me access to the more thoughtful, reflective parts of me. What if I just messed all of that up by asking her out?

So I delayed. I thought maybe I should never bring it up again. I passed the time reading her poetry on MySpace, getting lost in her words. For a brief moment, I convinced myself that maybe I should call her and say, "Never mind on that whole date thing." I couldn't shake the feeling that, in a date setting, in a setting where I had to be vulnerable enough to reveal how I felt, I would freeze. I'd have no armour to fall back on, since she already knew that the loudmouth persona was bullshit.

And freeze I did. On our date, we went to Copper Penny, a casual dining joint where I was not casual—or, for that matter, dining. I spent the whole meal avoiding her gaze, unable to speak a complete sentence. I ordered garlic bread (*why?????*) and when I noticed that cutting it with the provided knife left crumbs on the cutting board, I *simply stopped cutting* and stared at it for 4–5 minutes.

I walked her home and ended our date earlier than I wanted to. "I have to go home or my parents will get mad," I told her, and felt a stab of humiliation. What an incredibly *young* thing to say, I thought to myself. But the reality was that I was anxious about making it home so I didn't incur my parents' wrath.

A few weeks later, we found ourselves at the same party, a crowded affair in the basement of Sandy Gibson's house. And the thing about Sandy Gibson's house is: the ceiling of the basement kissed the top of my head. And Sandy liked to fit 30–40 more people in there than a reasonable person would.

It was warm and unpleasant in the basement, so I asked Emily if she'd take a walk with me. We lapped the block holding hands and talking into the night. I told her about the freedom I felt with her. I told her I resented how much my parents loomed over me. How if it weren't for them, I might be at another university right now, and how I felt the weight of their expectations. She told me about a hometown she needed to escape; about how she knew she needed to get out of there. Long looks and gentle hand squeezes deepened the night, deepened each other's company.

This was just the beginning. Every day after, we receded from the world and deeper into each other. We went for walks and revealed our wounds and fears. We sped past our cellphone plans' allotments of minutes, falling asleep on the phone with each other. I waited for her by the steps outside her work for a brief kiss, and she never made a big deal that I could only meet for nine minutes before catching the last bus home so as not to upset my parents. She just treasured the time we had.

In fact, Emily seemed less interested in my neuroses about what my parents would say, and more interested in me—which was novel because I only understood myself through those restrictions. It is a profound, transformative gift to have someone see you as you'd like to be seen, even if you don't see yourself that way.

We came up with workarounds to spend more time together. If I took a cab at 10:03, I could be home by 10:26, which was the same time the bus got me home— and we'd get a whole extra twenty-two minutes together. If I took the earliest bus to campus, I could be at her door for 7:25 a.m., and we could pretend we just woke up together. For Valentine's Day, we rented a fancy hotel suite, knowing I couldn't spend the night. She made space for me to be with her in whatever ways I could.

If Emily was bothered by my anxiety about not upsetting my parents, she never showed it. She just listened. We reacted to school pressures, roommate pressures, parent pressures, by finding each other, always. We started building a language of touch and laughter and joy and tears. We escaped into our own world, where only our dreams mattered. We started going somewhere only we knew.

NINE

House of Tears

Here's how death works in Sudan: following the passing of a loved one, a house is chosen as *beit albika'*, literally "the house of tears." This is not a metaphor—it will be the structure that contains the majority of the tears shed over the dead.

At first, the tears are informal: close family, gathered, bereft, torn. They cry together. Then no one knows how, because no one thinks to write these things down, but word begins to spread; the people in that house have had a *musseiba*—a calamity—and that's where the house of tears will be established.

As word spreads, people come. *Beit albika'* is serious business, and you do not delay arriving to add your tears to the house of tears. Part of this is functional—Islamic norms dictate that the dead be buried as soon as possible, and oftentimes this doesn't mean "later today," it means "within an hour or two." Friends and family coming to mourn know to gather quickly, to leave work or other life distractions immediately, if they want to witness the burial.

Next comes the formal part: a tented, seated area is established in front of the home, big enough to block the whole street. I'm sure someone makes the call to the tent place or whatever, but it seems to happen seamlessly— the tent just *appears*, and takes up space. There is to be no such trivial thing as through-traffic. Cars turn around if they see the mourning tent; they know that their inconvenience is secondary to this family's suffering.

The tent is both a visual cue that *hey, someone died here* and a gendered divider of mourning. The men sit in the tent and they drink tea with no milk, and they speak in austere tones, recite the same verse of the Qur'an with their hands stretched in prayer, and say phrases like *"Inna lillahi wa inna ilayhi raji'un"* ("We belong to God, and to Him we shall return") and *"Aldawam lillah wahdahu"* ("Permanence belongs only to God") and *"Sabber Allah"* ("God grants patience").

They say these words stoically and grimly every time someone new walks into the room, and every time they speak with a friend they haven't comforted yet, and every time they introduce themselves to a stranger sharing the tent in front of the house of tears. They know to keep saying these words because they act like a balm on the grieving soul. They are trying to heal one another.

The women, by contrast, wail. They sob and scream and ache loudly. Their bodies shake with crying. It is the sound that punctuates every moment of *beit albika'*. An uncontrollable agony. Every time a new woman enters the house of tears, she clasps the women around her by the shoulders and she looks them directly in the eyes and they cry together. They cry until you think there are no more tears left, and then the next woman enters, and they all start again.

The wailing is always loudest in the hallway leading into the largest room, where a bottleneck of weeping creates a wall of sound that ricochets off the sides and compounds and compounds until you think the structure will shatter at the force of the cries. But it never does.

A house of tears goes on for days. The tent remains fixed outside for a week or two, long after the burial, because a house of tears is an endless stream. In this stream, it is men talking gravely and women crying, and to the outsider, it always looks like the house of tears can't fit any more people, but on the inside, if you've come to mourn, there is always room for your grief.

∨

I say that I am fluent in Arabic, but this is partially a lie. The full truth is my grasp is a bit stunted: when I speak Arabic, I am a child. My predominant emotion is angst. I left Sudan at the outset of adolescence. In Canada, I mostly spoke the language with my strict parents, who were getting mad at me for seeking a freedom they thought was too Canadian and not Sudanese enough— like, say, asking to stay out past 9 p.m.

This means that, in Arabic, I am very good and very well-practised at asking for permission, sulking when I don't get it, and very bad at everything else. My Arabic is forever suspended in that place—I don't know how to be a fully grown adult in Arabic. I don't know how to reveal the inner workings of my brain in Arabic.

English, though, is a different story. My borders expanded in Canada, my language stretched here, and I was forced to find words for expressing the internal storms of teenagehood and young adulthood. That means I can illustrate for you the depths of my sadness and the heights of my joy by stringing together a few sentences. This is nice to do, yes, but it also has another function: it means I don't have to be alone. You can share in my emotions with me. That, ultimately, is the whole point of language, isn't it? To lessen the crushing burden of existence by creating a tiny bridge between us. I make some sounds, and you feel seen and understood and less lonely.

Arabic is the hometown I left long ago; I know how to traverse in it, all the while aware of the ways it cannot contain me. Aware that I've developed modes of being and ways of expressing myself that do not fit within its walls. I roam its streets, at once comfortable and acutely aware of my estrangement from it and my loneliness in it.

Not having the words is akin to not having pieces of the map: you know that something exists in these spots but you haven't the slightest idea how to describe it. And so while I have spent time looking inward in English, I don't have the words to do that in Arabic. I don't know how to say what I don't know how to say, and I am shattered by its unknowability. I am a half-formed being made up of half-formed thoughts.

In English, I am familiar with grief's devastating contours. In Arabic, it's a collection of incoherent thoughts. As I got older, emotional landscapes like grief got oceans deeper and more profound, but only in one language. So when someone in my family dies, I am both more aware of the full range of my sorrow *and* less able to express its colours to my family in Arabic.

∨

The first time death wrecked me, I was ten years old and I lost the person I loved most in the world. But when you're that young, you don't know words like *cataclysmic*, you just know that you've been dealt a blow from which you'll never quite recover.

The first thing you need to know about my grandmother, my *haboba*, is that she was the single best human to ever live. She was warm and she was gentle and she was beautiful, and when she was stern, it was the right amount, the amount that didn't make you go into a shame spiral. Her hands were love, her fragile touch was never judgemental. She was an extraordinary reader of people. She understood the kind of person you were within a split second of meeting you, and still greeted the best version of you. Plus, I was her favourite person, so that colours my judgement a little.

It's customary here to describe a person's physical appearance, which for her might include words like *diminutive* and *frail* and *bespectacled*, but to me she was made of light. She radiated light. It was immediately obvious to anyone who ever met her that her instinct always tended toward kindness; her disposition always toward being generous.

But she wasn't just generous, she was relentlessly so. For example, she would never let on that she knew the rest of the family found my aunt Aisha difficult to get along with, and she pretended not to notice when everyone distanced themselves from her. But Haboba, the brilliant conductor of love that she was, knew how to keep my aunt from drifting away: every year, when Ramadan approached, she would say, "Take me to Aisha's house." And she stayed there for the whole month, forcing the rest of us to come visit my aunt's house if we wanted to see Haboba during an occasion traditionally reserved for spending time with family. My grandmother would bring the family together without ever saying this was her plan. It was her way of leaving the light on for us to find one another, without her saying a word. This was the wisdom of her tenderness.

The day she died is still the worst day of my life.

∨

I used to think that it was utterly offensive that Christians believed if you are good and you die, then you go to heaven.

The version I grew up with is quite different. *No one* goes to heaven or hell when they die—that part doesn't happen until Judgement Day, which, depending on who you ask is either coming any minute now or about 1,500 or so years away.

In the meantime, I was told, after you're buried, two angels descend from the heavens and ask you three questions: What did you believe when you were in the world? Who was your God? And who was his prophet?

If you answer all three correctly, you get a special prize: the angels open a window through which you can feel heaven's breeze, so that your days in the grave are comfortable until Judgement Day arrives. If you get the answers wrong, you are tortured in the grave until the big day comes, when you are transferred to hell for some higher-order torturing.

Because the grave is seen as a journey between life and the afterlife, when someone dies it is common to pray for the deceased to have patience and strength for the grave-questioning. More importantly, every single time someone mentions the name of a person who died—and this applies forever—you say *"Allah yarhamu"* or "God forgive them."

Long after you die, every time you are spoken of, everyone who knew you is pleading your case to God. Meanwhile, you're just waiting.

❤

The day my grandmother died, I held her hand. We got the call that she was probably not going to make it through the night, so we made our way to her bedside, in a room that used to be my room, in a house we had left long ago.

It's strange, seeing a space you're intimately familiar with in a context like this: here was the room I'd slept in, in the house where I learned to crawl, where I'd watched the *Ninja Turtles*, but we no longer lived here, and this room had been transformed for my grandmother's comfort.

My aunt Jazz, my favourite aunt, was giving her mother droplets of water with a spoon, as death stood by checking her watch. We could see my grandmother's chest slightly rise and slightly fall, but she was not responding to anyone or anything.

Jazz told Haboba that I had entered the room, and Haboba's hand, for the first time in hours, moved: her fingers rose and reached for me. Her hand, so soft and fragile, as if there were no bones, seemed to wave off death itself and clasp mine. I held it gently between my palms, and though all logic says she was probably too weak for this to have happened, my memory swears that I saw her smiling. And then—

It was 1 a.m. in Khartoum, 7 p.m. in Kingston when we called my dad. He was just waking up before a night shift when we told him. I can't say that I remember how the call went. I remember saying "*Inna lillahi wa inna ilayhi raji'un*" over and over, calmly and steadily. I remember that I knew to keep saying the words and I remember they fell like a balm on a grieving soul.

∨

My uncle Mustafa raised me after my father left Sudan. He wouldn't put it that way—to him, he was just looking after his baby sister and her little boy in the temporary absence of his brother-in-law.

But to me, he was the whole world.

We called him Foofoo affectionately, and rarely by his name. He was a joyful figure with a mirthful laugh and a mischievous smile. He didn't pray often and he occasionally drank alcohol(!), but he fasted during Ramadan—which made him an anomaly. He was political and an intellectual, and could quote Kant and Marx and Hegel in Arabic by heart.

Foofoo made me love books and ideas, and he wouldn't let me get away with a half-formed thought. We read mystery and adventure novels together, and we talked about them and the ideas in them. When he brought home a new one, he made an event out of the reveal—but I had to work for it. He'd get home and deliberately act suspicious, like he was hiding something, and pretend he was guarding his briefcase closely. Then he'd go along as I concocted elaborate schemes to get access to his bag ("Uncle, a stray dog has wandered in the yard, I'm scared, can you go let it out?") and steal the new book. After he caught me running away with my bounty, he'd graciously let me read it first. We talked about ideas that I didn't understand when I was little—later, replaying the memories, I would realize that Foofoo was trying to introduce me to the concept of the self, or enlightenment, or colonialism. He was always talking to me about politics, encouraging me to question the repressive regime, and also planting the seed early that capitalism is not the answer to Sudan's woes. All I wanted to do, all the time, was listen to Foofoo. I have fragments of language for so many heady ideas because of Foofoo.

In any room, he was either the loudest laugh or the reason for it. He adored music and poetry and hosting gatherings to talk about music and poetry. Everyone who knew him would say that he was larger than life.

He was also just a big man. For most of his life, Foofoo weighed over five hundred pounds. His gut stretched out so far in front of him that he developed a peculiar stride, leaning back as he walked as though, if he didn't, he would simply topple over onto his front from the force of the weight.

He wasn't just large—he was cautionary-tale fat. Around the dinner table, going for seconds meant receiving a warning that if I didn't want to "end up like Foofoo" I'd better leave it alone. If it bothered him, Foofoo never showed it. He would just grin and slip me the extra piece of bread I was reaching for.

Leaving Sudan was hard. Leaving Foofoo was the hardest.

❧

"Complications of diabetes" is not a very good descriptor. Foofoo had diabetes—of course he had diabetes—but it was undiagnosed until a few days before his death. It was discovered when he injured his leg, accidentally pushing it into an exposed nail. The injury was the instigator; the diabetes the reason why his body couldn't properly deal with it.

They operated, sure, but it was functionally too late. On July 13, 2013, Foofoo died.

I was at work when I found out. You know those calls when you look down at your phone and see who's calling, and for some reason it feels like an off time for that person's call? This was one of those. My mother called, and just as my eye caught the ringing phone, it went to voicemail. Then I heard the message and my world went black.

"Oh, my heart . . . my world . . . Your uncle . . . our protector, who loved us so much, who looked after us . . . He's gone." Those were the words I could make out from the distressed voice.

I called her back. Her first word was *ilhaqni*, which docs not have a direct translation in English. Its root word, *ilhaq*, roughly means "hurry, before it's too late." But *ilhaqni* specifically applies to a person in crisis—it means "hurry, I need you, I am out of my depth." It connotes an urgency not unlike if you'd fallen through the ice. It's a word for needing another person. It's a word for when you can't save yourself.

I don't remember when I left work, or when I got into a car (or bus?) to go to my mom who was two and a half hours away. I don't remember how I got there, but I remember that at a certain point, at the door of my mom's apartment, it occurred to me that I was about to enter, for the first time since arriving in Canada, a house of tears.

Women came in and out of the apartment—far fewer than there would be in Sudan—and they held each other's shoulders and they wept together. I was shaken and I was grieving and I was untethered. But I did not speak Arabic as fluidly and fluently and musically as I used to. So I did not speak, because my words offered no solace.

v

Funerals in English are tidy, quiet affairs. The tenor of sadness is different when the grief has to be contained. In the immediate aftermath of death, for the living there's a lot of talk of "being strong," as though strength is grieving without letting it destroy you. As though grief is a dam, and your job is to make sure it doesn't burst.

In other words, funerals in English are also, a little bit, about moving on. About not coming undone despite your *musseiba*. About taming the wild horses of mourning. At these funerals, people do what they can to project at least the *idea* that they will, after some time, be okay. They speak about work or children or life or the news. They have little sandwiches and they hang their heads in sadness, but there is no deafening wall of hysterical crying. There may be tears in your house, but it is not a house of tears.

At first, the silence of these funerals freaked me out. I looked for the signs of grief I knew—I looked for the wailing—but I found only a quiet despair. At the funeral for a friend's father, it struck me that people attending funerals in English are inhabiting their own individual universes of grief. They may vary in intensity, but their borders are internal.

This has its advantages: it allows you to poke around your emotions in your head, circle them, explore their shape. It allows you to wade deeper into yourself, perhaps visit a corner you've never seen, and let death illuminate your interior landscape. When you've sat long enough with the grief, you can maybe even share it with other people. This is called "processing." Your brain learns to make sense of the world without the departed.

The main disadvantage, though, is that this is a spectacularly lonely order of operations. There are few ways to collectively heal in the wake of a loss. You're left largely to fight your own war.

ᴠ

My mother's cousin, who I've called my aunt for my whole life, didn't have very long to live when she came to live with Mama. Cancer is cruel like that. The pair spent my aunt's last weeks talking and laughing and reminiscing about their childhood in Sudan, when she wasn't going to chemo or gingerly walking to her fifty-eighth medical appointment of the week.

The cancer had spread, they said, and there was nothing they could do. *Ilhaqni*—that word again. My aunt died in my mother's arms on her couch. Once again, another makeshift *beit albika'*, one that bore some resemblance to the ones in Sudan. Except the cars do not find another road here, and life's pace does not stop when death happens, so the house of tears was abbreviated.

For months after, my mom couldn't bear to look at the couch, couldn't bear to go outside, couldn't bear to stay indoors. Despite this, she was surprised when her doctor suggested she might be depressed. When I asked her how she felt about this, she said with nonchalance, "I'm not depressed, I just wish I could be in Sudan to cry properly with the rest of my family so I can *itfesha*."

Itfesha is another of those Sudanese-dialect Arabic words with no precise translation. The closest I can get is this: it means to untangle the knot in your soul, to release the tension in your body, to unclench the grip of the world on your heart. For my mom, being in a proper *beit albika'*, filled with people who grieve the way she does, who let themselves mourn by wailing and building a symphony of devastation—that's the way to process loss.

∨

And so I don't have an opportunity to *itfesha*. Building an inner life in English while my Arabic stalls has meant the transformation of grief from something I wrap my mind around communally, through ritual and repeating words that give comfort, to an object that exists in my head. A terrain that I share with no one. Something to "process."

This, on its own, is not a bad thing. Knowing how you grieve and what to look for when you aren't coping are powerful tools. In loss, I know how to let death illuminate the dark woods inside.

But I've never felt as half-formed as I did trying to share with my mother what Foofoo meant to me, my thoughts trapped in one language as her grief poured out in another. We'd both lost a pole of our worlds—but saying that, in English, would provide no reprieve from the storms of mourning.

After the women came and went, after the Canadian version of *beit albika'* was dismantled far too soon, I searched for the words to tell my mom that I, too, was unmoored by the loss. That I missed Foofoo more than anything, that I never stopped thinking about him, that I never will.

But none of these thoughts came out.

Instead, we sat across from each other, silent and shipwrecked in the same wild ocean. We just sat.

TEN

The O.C.

"The amorous subject," writes Roland Barthes in *A Lover's Discourse: Fragments*, "lives in the belief that the loved object does love him but does not tell him so." If you ask me, that's just a fancy way of saying that having a crush makes you lose touch with reality.

This belief that somewhere, somehow, your "loved object" is also crushing on you *but just can't tell you* is the very engine of the crush, which is the most unnerving of romantic entanglements. Crushes are unhinged. They are unrestrained chaos. How do you capture the dynamics of the crush? If the distance between two magnets hurtling toward each other is a magnetic field, what do we call the space between a magnet and all the things it does not attract? I'm asking for a friend. That friend is me.

For the first three years in Canada, I crushed a lot. I crushed all the time, unprovoked, and at the faintest sign of interest. I was a professional crusher. I'd received all my crush training at the private school I attended in Khartoum, where boys and girls were separated. We took the same buses to and from school, but classes and recesses were divided. As a result, I spent my lunches staring at the wall that separated me from Hiba or Neda or Nahid.

I'd replay the tape in my head—had Hiba shared her Pepsi with me on the bus because she liked me? Neda had definitely turned around and hit me for no reason because she was in love with me. Before you knew it, I'd put 10,000 hours into being an "amorous subject." If sustaining a crush were an Olympic event, I would have medalled.

So, by the time I moved to Kingston and was in the first co-ed classes of my life, I had a lot of practice. Except I now felt trapped by these crushes, because while I was consumed by the flames I did not have the language to say so. How could I tell Kaitlin that when I made her laugh, I became alive in ways I didn't know possible? How do I tell Nadine that I loved how she drew hearts on the bottoms of her jeans, and it made me want to draw them, too? I'd have loved to send hints to Mariam that I knew she sharpened my pencil because she was madly in love with me, but I literally had no idea how to do that. How do you flirt in this unromantic language? Because if I was crushing, and my crush was for sure crushing on me back (and why wouldn't she be!!!!), then the real crisis at work was that we simply couldn't tell each other.

So, I had all this highly refined, weapons-grade crushing energy, and I had to just walk around with it. I had to steal glimpses at Nicole playing Weezer on her guitar and pretend I was too mesmerized to speak, because I literally did not have the words.

That is, until the summer of 2003, when lightning struck and I was changed forever: *The O.C.* premiered on Fox. Do you remember where you were when *The O.C.* premiered? Of course you don't. No one seems to know the answer to this question because few people seem to carry *The O.C.* with them all the time. For them, *The O.C.* is little more than a distant memory of a time gone by. Those who do remember it might scoff at its melo-dramatics, not the way it defined an era of television.

Me, I remember *The O.C.* because it just so happened to arrive as I was clearing the diving board, plunging into the ice-cold pool of adolescence. This could've been *any* show—others report the same full-body jolt with *Felicity* or *Sex and the City* or *Charmed* or *90210*—but for me, it was *The O.C.*

The summer *The O.C.* landed, I was at a turning point. I had spent the last three years trying to learn English. That year, I'd had my *first* full thought in English. I was also on the precipice of a new challenge: I had enrolled myself in a hands-on education program where fifteen students were tasked with running a radio station.

Three years before, I couldn't speak the language. Now, I was going to try to talk on live radio *for school credit*. The past three years had been about treading water. Now it was time to go swimming in the deep end.

Luckily for me, I didn't have to do this alone. I had Ryan, Marissa, Seth, and Summer. *The O.C.* unlocked the puzzle of who I wanted to become. But we'll get to that.

❧

To speak and to be understood is a freedom. It is perhaps *the* most fundamental freedom. To summon words *intentionally*, and have another person understand your meaning and connect with it, is to be unbound.

Conversely, without it, a part of you is caged. You feel betrayed by a spotty brain-tongue connection. And you notice when others don't catch your full drift. Maybe it's the context of what you mean; maybe it's the inflection in your voice; maybe it's undercutting yourself by putting the emphasis on the wrong syllable.

This trapped feeling is far more acute when you move in a language that isn't your own. There are intricacies and subtleties that matter a great deal to communicating. Without them, your meaning is stuck in your throat. This is how I felt after arriving in Canada, where I had to translate simple thoughts into English, with all the added social cues, before I could get them past my lips.

This translation work is labour. It's time and effort spent trying to wrangle unruly words that won't fit in your mouth. God, have you tried to say "parallelogram"? Have you tried to differentiate it from a rhombus? When will I ever need to say "parallelogram?" Anyway: it's mental gymnastics, and the only reward is blank looks on the faces of people who can tell you're trying to say *something* but hear another. *Maybe I messed up the syntax? Maybe my pronunciation was off and now I have to spend twenty minutes convincing you I'm not stupid? Damn, I can't believe some people can just* speak *and be understood. The luxury!*

The torture of suspended meaning was what awaited me after moving to Canada. In my first month here, one day on the playground, as I came down the slide, I found myself face to face with a pretty girl in a red dress and her friend in jean overalls.

"Hey kid," she called out. "What's your name?" Somehow, I found myself spelling my last name to the pair. *Eh. Bee. Dee. Ee. Ell. Emm. Eh. Etch.* "What?" *Etch.* They exchanged a look. *Etch, etch, etch,* I repeated. "Ooooooh. It's *aitch.* You don't know how to say it." Her friend slid down the slide and shrugged. "He doesn't know how to say it," the girl in the red dress said to the other girl, speaking about me as though I no longer existed. I went home with a feeling that didn't yet have a name in my limited English.

H is for *humiliation.*

∨

2003 was a big year for shows that would go on to reshape TV. *The Bachelorette, America's Next Top Model,* and *The Ellen Degeneres Show* launched within months of each other and would go on to have a colossal effect on how we make TV. *Chappelle's Show* changed comedy forever. Pamela Anderson's *Stripperella* launched that year too, but that's neither here nor there. And then you had *The O.C.*

Like all soaps before it, *The O.C.* relies on constantly torqued stakes. There's this roughneck kid, Ryan Atwood

(Ben McKenzie), who somehow gets taken in by Sandy Cohen (Peter Gallagher), a well-eyebrowed Jewish public defender who's married to Kirsten (Kelly Rowan), who comes from Serious Money. The lovely have-it-all couple have a quirky son, Seth (Adam Brody), because of course they do. He wouldn't like it very much if you called him nerdy, but let us make a habit of speaking truth to power: he's nerdy.

The engine of the show is Ryan being out of place in a rich neighbourhood in Newport Beach. Ryan's lower-class upbringing makes him uncomfortable in the moneyed mansions of the O.C., which makes him an odd fit with everyone—except for the idealistic Cohen family, who are, yes, rich, but also *good,* thank you very much.

But show descriptions are boring, so I want you to put down this book and google the scene where Ryan sees Marissa waiting outside for the first time; and then the scene where Seth is being bullied by the puka-necklaced Luke, and Ryan intervenes, only to get knocked out by Luke, who delivers the godawful and now-iconic line "Welcome to the O.C., bitch." There, you're caught up.

In 2003, I found myself in another unfamiliar situation. I'd signed up for what my local school board called a "focus program"—where students got to participate in non-classroom education for credit. But the truth is, I didn't actually know what a focus program *was*. The brochure came to my school, and I listened to the radio constantly, so I liked the idea of doing a brief extracurricular workshop on how to do radio. I thought maybe I could skip math for a week or something.

As it turned out, I'd accidentally signed up for a whole semester of programming a radio station with fourteen other students, at a *different school*, halfway across town. CKVI 91.9 FM, The Cave, is a real radio station you can tune into right now in Kingston—but only downtown Kingston, since its signal is profoundly weak—and you will hear high school students who program, write, and host radio shows all day.

I had to go to a school that was new to me, and spend every day learning how to make radio. I'd only just begun to feel comfortable with the mishmash of friends I'd assembled in one school who could cope with my English. Oops—seems I'd gone and signed up for a whole new set of people.

∨

All anyone could talk about in fall 2003 was *The O.C.* There was a buzz around the show that was larger than life, with audiences hanging on every word, hooked in by every cliffhanger in the lives of these hot, dumb, sometimes kind and sometimes mean white people. In the hallways, you'd catch snippets of conversations: "What's the deal with Ryan's brother?" "Seth is actually too hot for Summer," "Mrs. Cohen is hot as hell" (that last one was me).

It was the nascent days of social media, and the last era before texting took over, so the conversation mostly took place in person or on MSN Messenger. People watched *The O.C.* together over Messenger, embroiled in a breathless fandom.

One particularly cool thing about this giant cultural conversation: I could actually participate. After three years of observing people in my new home, three years of my tongue acclimating to the way white Kingstonians spoke English, I was ready to try on a voice. For the first time since arriving in Canada, they couldn't tell that all I thought about was that I didn't belong. For the first time, I kinda did.

For me and my permanent crush-affliction, this opened up new worlds. I could have inside jokes with Lucy, the goth girl with the big toothy smile and always-mismatched socks. I could lightly tease Marla without it sounding too mean, because the thing with teasing is that there's a delicate line between "charming" and "asshole." So much of crush communication is about tone, and I could finally spend time working on that instead of being hampered by the dominant anxiety that I was going to choose the wrong word at the perfect moment. That all of this dovetailed with *The O.C.* was a godsend.

The chief contribution of *The O.C.* is pouty lips. The next important contribution of *The O.C.* is a character study of crush life. The show was a masterclass in yearning—the gold standard of pining. How else could you explain how audiences desperately begged for Seth and Summer to take off? The ways Seth fell apart at the sight of Summer; how one look from her put him back together? And while Ryan and Marissa went through turmoil, I was ready to be seen as something more than the guy who couldn't speak English well. To drive a wrecking ball through the idea that my accent was my personality. To *feel* fifteen, with all its delicious three-dimensional complexity.

The O.C. also happened to coincide with a major crush on a girl we'll call Vanessa. She was beautiful, sweet, and soft-spoken. She could make any conversation feel like a hushed secret, just for us to know. She dotted every *i* with a heart. And, as happens when you're fifteen and have a crush, I discovered I could listen to her voice or read her words for hours.

My feelings for her grew with every word we exchanged, until my primary identity slowly ceased to be "immigrant kid" and became "teenager with a crush." And what a relief this identity change was—to not feel foreignness constantly, but instead just feel a universal longing.

∨

If *The O.C.* was a vast expanse of emotions, its soundtrack was meant to be your map. Josh Schwartz, who created the show, said he wanted the music to "feel like a character." He succeeded to a stunning level: even *The O.C.*'s most devoted fans remember the soundtrack better than they remember the plot.

There's the scene where Seth dances in his bathrobe to Eels' "Saturday Morning." There's the breakup scene set to Youth Group's cover of "Forever Young." A montage of characters at a crossroads, set to Electric President's "Insomnia." *The O.C.* understood the way music encodes memories and brings you closer to inhabiting characters.

The show was loaded with these moments: perfectly matched songs and scenes. Even now, the opening notes of these songs can trigger a flood of memories. Famously, there's the SNL-parodied shooting scene, set to Imogen Heap's "Hide and Seek," now forever known as "Mmm Whatcha Say."

Two decades later, the show is widely credited for the launch of pop culture's mid-aughts indie music moment. Bands like Death Cab for Cutie and Spoon and Rooney, who were killing it on indie radio, made the jump to proper pop stardom because of *The O.C.* The show's soundtracks were a portal to cool. And I could buy cool for $17.99 at the local Sunrise Records.

∨

I was, regrettably, the second to arrive at the radio station for the first day of the semester. The teacher, a cheerful dude named Mr. Power, greeted me and the other early bird, Ferris, with endless enthusiasm—and also the news that, since we were there early, we'd have to deliver the morning broadcast, a short few minutes to introduce the day on-air.

The thing about being able to trust words is that it's a luxury. Trusting the right words to come out in the right order in the right way was not something I could take for granted, because I hadn't always had this option in English. So that morning, asked to get on the mic, I simply froze.

I stumbled through an awkward weather forecast—the kind you'd hear from someone who's never heard a weather forecast before—and wore my shame about my performance. Ferris, a drama class star who arrived fully formed and ready to command your attention, rescued me. If he was worried about what the hell I was doing in a program where I'd have to talk for credit, he didn't show it.

Then, while we were introducing ourselves to each other, *The O.C.* came up. It came up casually, in the organic way the biggest things on TV bubble up in high school conversations. Except *on this*, I had something to say. I didn't have to express my love for the show in particularly sophisticated words—but that wasn't necessary: a conversation was happening, and I could just be part of it in an uncomplicated way.

Week by week, episode after episode, I grew more confident. I'd overhear conversations about the show in the school cafeteria, and offer thoughts to complete strangers because I knew we could bond over how regularly our minds were being blown by the show's fast developments.

Because of *The O.C.*, I started to trust words to tell the story in my head, to at last share my thoughts on something other people had thoughts about. This was a whole new world.

❖

Seth Cohen rewrote the rules for geeks on TV.

, The character was far from the first TV super-nerd, but he was the most significant geek on TV in the twenty-first century. To get the credentials out of the way: Seth drew superheroes and listened to weird indie bands no one around him had heard of; he read Chuck Klosterman *and talked about it*; he carried comic books around with him.

But the smart writing of the show allowed Seth to also be fully human—which is to say, to have all the markers of nerdiness and yet never have that be the punchline. He was allowed to fall in love and be brave and be wistful and reject and be rejected. And, most importantly, he was written as someone who was worthy of love, and that depiction was shown to a mass audience of millions, during prime time.

His bona fides went deeper than surface-level references to what awkward nerds are supposed to like: Seth was occasionally allowed to show his deep love of things that he had no one to talk about with, like when he excitedly mentioned authors that only genuinely cool, weird kids would know. In that way, the show arrived at a dimension of geekdom that was beyond the superficial: he was lonely and eager to share himself, too.

So many of the depictions of nerds that followed Seth tried to copy what *The O.C.* did—but copied the wrong thing. They'd copy Seth's trademark snark, but chalk it up to superiority (*The Big Bang Theory*) instead of loneliness. They'd copy his awkwardness, but chalk it up to social ineptitude (*The IT Crowd*) instead of Seth's guarded approach toward people who have long pretended he doesn't exist.

In so many shows, the geekiness is the gimmick. That's where the interrogation ends. In *The O.C.*, Seth's outsider behaviour isn't just in full colour—it has consequences, too. The stakes are high when he's vulnerable, when he makes an effort to connect, to try to make someone laugh. It's little wonder that people fell in love with the character.

The nerd figure and the archetypal immigrant share the outsider identity. But it's what *The O.C.* does with this framing that matters: Seth offers a cerebral, intimate look at the ways we are misunderstood when we extend ourselves and make a connection. How the little moments break your heart.

⌄

I mean, is it geeky to write thousands of words in emails to your crush every day? Yeah, maybe. But consider this: Vanessa was Muslim too, and I knew that because of the similarities between our home lives and our strict parents, my best shot at getting her attention was with words. So I wrote her words. Thousands of them, over dozens of emails. I trusted the words to tell the story.

Over episodes of *The O.C.*, I'd watch a character who believed in his bones that his words were the only thing he could offer the woman he longed for, hoping that was enough. And, well, look—I unabashedly tried to replicate that feeling. I'd put *Music from the O.C.: Mix 1* on and let the keystrokes fly.

Music can bring your softest, most vulnerable self to the surface. And it's that self that poured out onto the screen. I put on Joseph Arthur's "Honey and the Moon," and recalled the vulnerability on Ryan's face in the pilot as he looks back at Marissa. Nada Surf's "If You Leave" took me to Seth's uncharacteristic courage in chasing a love interest to the airport. Jem's airy cover of Paul McCartney's "Maybe I'm Amazed" made me picture Ryan and Marissa sharing what could be a fragile final dance.

These songs were witness to me grasping for romance for the first time since arriving in Canada. They were companions, holding my hand as I found the words. And find them I did. Each email I'd send contained about 4,000 words, or 40,000 new ways for me to escape being just The Kid Not From Here. *The O.C.*'s soundtrack gave me that.

I treated *The O.C.* as a living document of what to do when you're consumed by a crush. I came to the TV screen each week wild and disassembled, eager for something that would give me shape and structure and voice. An idea of how to proceed. A framework, if you will: a scaffolding for how to relate. *How can I be tender in this language? How do I express hints of desire?* Above all, perhaps the show could teach me how to be understood by one specific person.

So this is how a mostly-forgotten teen drama came to be the vehicle for being seen. It enabled me to transform my idea of myself—from a person who was never going to fit in, to a teen who could have a chill conversation about a show; a teen who was also adrift, hopelessly, in a crush. In other words: to feel like I belonged.

The O.C. was, ultimately, a blip in TV history. But it opened the door for an outsider to be understood socially, emotionally, romantically. Its music and tone gave me access I didn't have. It stayed with me for a brief but transformative stretch.

Peter Gallagher once told a reporter that when he encountered the script for *The O.C.*, he thought: "In that recently post-9/11 America . . . it was exactly the right story to be telling . . . that was powerful in an era with a kind of xenophobia, a kind of looking-over-your-shoulder and getting small and angry, sort of creeping into the PATRIOT Act-fueled environment." He was describing the ways these characters revealed themselves to strangers, and trusted the process to create beauty.

Maybe the journey from being an outsider to something recognizable is a journey of allowing yourself to be transformed, of letting others affect you. That was Ryan's journey. And I didn't know it then, but *The O.C.* was my guide on the same trip.

❯

I returned to my regular school after the focus program much more confident in what I had to offer, having shed the heavy insecurity of not feeling understood. Then, about halfway through that semester, I found out that I'd got a job I really wanted.

That job was back at the radio station. Out of the two cohorts that had been through the program that year, I was one of just two students selected to run the station during the summer. I'd be splitting duties with the other student, each of us taking half of the season. Me, the one who couldn't read the weather, would have a full-time job as the only person on-air for two months.

Every day, I arrived at 7:30 a.m., and I hosted every show on the schedule until about 5 p.m. I often chuckled, remembering my nerves, my lack of trust in words when I'd started there at the beginning of the school year. I programmed everything. Blues shows and jazz shows, punk shows and hip hop shows—and in between songs, I talked and talked, the words dancing on my tongue like they'd always belonged there.

Certain that no one was listening, I sometimes let the odd inappropriate word slip out ("Now that's a fuckin' song," I'd say over Led Zeppelin's "Fool in the Rain"). Every time I did so, the station's phone rang—and it was almost always the same elderly man, who'd say "I heard that! Please tell whoever is on-air to watch his language."

On occasion, I would be short a few minutes on a show, so I kept a small stack of CDs next to the control board as a safety blanket. If I could see that I wasn't going to make it to the next time marker, I'd reach over and grab *Music from the O.C.: Mix 2* and skip straight to track no. 6.

As the slide guitar melted into the bass, and Patrick Park sang, "I know ugliness / Now show me something pretty," my shoulders would drop. I imagined the softness of being understood, transmitted over radio waves. I imagined Vanessa listening. I imagined an audience of one. And we just talked.

ELEVEN

Roads (Part IV)

The night my mother went into hospital with a heart problem, I didn't hear the phone. I was four blocks away from Kingston General, in Emily's student house, tending to her. She was in the throes of a vicious bout of mono.

We'd been dating for six months or so, a nascent relationship already tested by the forces of my disapproving parents. The night she fell ill, I stayed by her side for hours, holding her clammy hands, handing her a bucket when she needed it, pulling her blanket tight as she shivered with the chills.

Anxious about leaving Emily, and watchful of the internal clock that said *Mama and Baba are going to be so mad that I'm not home yet*, I checked my phone at 11:30 p.m. Four missed calls, two voicemails from Baba. *Shit*.

In the voicemail, I instantly recognized his calm and admonishing tone, the tenor laced with the disappointment that immediately triggers guilt, the one that every parent has perfected. "Mama had a heart attack. We had to call the ambulance to come get her. Where are you? You better not be where I think you are."

My heart sank.

I arrived at the hospital twenty minutes later, to the sight of my mother connected to oxygen and half a dozen medical monitors. Her eyes were teary from the shock; her labouring breath and the beeps of the devices were the only sounds in the room. I collapsed at her bedside and stayed there all night, barely cognizant of the nurses and doctors coming in and out. I registered three things acutely: the feel of my mom's hands; the worry about Emily, who was alone and so ill; and the occasional icy glance from Baba. With every ping of the heart monitor, I felt the shame in me intensifying. I wasn't there when Mama needed me, and the silence in the room was going to be my reminder of this.

The next morning, sleepless, I returned to check on Emily briefly and waited with her until her parents arrived to take her to Hamilton, where she could recover under their care. I hoped the highway carrying her home would look after her.

Mama started recovering at home, and she was growing stronger every day. This was reassuring to me. A doctor also prescribed a small squad of heart medications. One of them, he said, would be her "permanent friend." He told her to never miss it—not ever in her life. This was serious business. But at least I could see Mama recovering. Laying eyes on someone you love can comfort your worst fears, even if that person is still frail.

Three hundred and thirty kilometres west, Emily's recovery was slow. Mono had debilitated her, and it left her bedridden for weeks; she was jaundiced and could barely eat. Her voice on the phone was hoarse, and her thoughts were foggy from being exhausted all the time. Everything exhausted her: sitting up, standing up, taking a shower, finishing sentences, concentrating on any task. She needed naps after every phone call because her illness was sapping all her strength. She had to hand her mother the phone often because she was feeling so weak.

I grew anxious about her, and hated the thought of her going through this without me. At the same time, I was attuned to the sting my absence had caused when Mama had her emergency, and it made the prospect of telling my parents that I was going to visit Emily that much more of a burden. I remembered Baba's voice on the phone, the way every word had felt sharp.

So, when I did decide to visit Emily to check on her, I knew I wasn't going to tell Mama and Baba.

I secured an early ride with a stranger and hit the 401 again. It was a multi-step plan, with a delicate balance. Everything had to go right. If we left at 8:30, I could make it to see Emily by noon, then hop on the bus to Toronto seventy-five minutes later, catch the connecting bus to Kingston an hour and a half after that, and be back before my parents ever knew I was gone. Easy-peasy. I trusted the highway to help me pull off this plan.

And the highway came through. For a brief moment, I got to hold the sickly love of my life. I held her withered frame and felt her spirits lifting. Our fingers interlaced, and we huddled together for as long as we could.

Later, as the bus peeled off the highway and onto the exit ramp in Kingston, I thanked the highway. I made it home in time for dinner, and my parents never suspected a thing.

❧

It can be tempting to speed on the 401, especially on a breezy spring day. But if you're just leaving Kingston, don't do it. About forty kilometres west, in Napanee, there's a particularly ambitious Ontario Provincial Police detachment. I don't have the numbers to verify their ambition, but I am armed with about a decade of anecdotal evidence that all adds up to the incontrovertible fact that they *will* get you.

The highway gently curves and winds around a Flying J gas station that looks about 2,000 years old. But listen to me. *Listen to me.* Two overpasses after the Flying J, in a little tucked-away spot, an OPP car will probably be waiting. They will probably have a radar gun trained on you. You will not notice they're there until they've measured your speed. If you're speeding, you will see the flashing lights in your rear-view before you've had a chance to brake and return to a legal speed. I don't want this for you.

∨

In the summer of 2009, tensions were about ready to boil over in my home. My parents, long resistant to my relationship with Emily, were coming to the realization that it was not a "phase."

Mama, ever the pragmatist, had pacified Baba into believing that I was "experimenting" and the relationship would soon come to an end. But now, two and a half years had passed, and if this was a phase, it sure wasn't showing signs of letting up.

Their strategy—not a good one, they'd admit now—
was to forbid out-of-town trips, in the hopes that this
might limit the time Emily and I spent together in the
summers between university years. The problem was
that I was now twenty-one, and being told something
was "forbidden" didn't feel like my jam.

This all came to a head before the wedding of a
friend, out of town. I let my parents know I planned to
attend, and I'd be gone for the weekend. It wasn't so
much a "can I go?" as it was an FYI. Mama thought I was
making up the trip in order to go visit Emily. Her
response was to say, "If you go on this trip, never ever
come back into my home again."

I had no reason to doubt her words. But I had also
grown tired of the limitations and red lines. So on a
warm August morning, I woke up early and made up my
mind. I packed my bags with the clothes I couldn't live
without. As I headed for the door, silence greeted me.
I felt tears welling up. Mama was drinking tea, her back
to me, while Baba was reading the news. I said, "I love
you, and I'm going. I can't miss my friend's wedding."

Mama straightened her back and turned around to
give me a challenging stare. She said nothing. I walked
toward the door, and whispered goodbye. As I grabbed

the handle, I heard Mama's voice. "You are no longer our son, and you will not be welcome here. Don't call me ever again."

I dragged my suitcase down the stairs of the apartment building, my legs shaking from the finality and certainty in Mama's voice. I pulled the suitcase across the parking lot, and headed to meet my ride to the wedding. I remember that, in its infinite wisdom, my Sony Ericsson decided it would score this moment of confusing heartbreak with "Alegría" from the Cirque du Soleil album. It's an overwhelming and melodramatic song about joy, so not exactly the soundtrack for leaving your parents forever. But with every step, every explosion of this thunderous song, my resolve grew. Sure, I was no longer speaking to the most important people in my life, but I had the clarity to know that this was their choice. Hot tears streamed down my face.

By the time the car hit the 401, I was taking account of what this new reality meant. Yes, I was fearful for the future—where the hell was I going to stay?!—but I couldn't deny the pulse of excitement coursing through my body. For the first time in my life, I would get a chance to set my own rules. So as we sped down the road, my heart danced.

Three days later, after I returned from the wedding and crashed on a friend's couch, Mama called me. "Why didn't you call?" she asked matter-of-factly.

I shouted, "Because you said never to call you again!"

Her voice softened. "You should've known I didn't mean it."

From that point on, I knew our relationship had changed, but we were going to be just fine.

❯

Everyone calls it the 401, but the highway's government name is the Macdonald-Cartier Freeway. Premier John Robarts gave the highway the name in 1965, to celebrate John A. Macdonald and George-Étienne Cartier, two of Canada's Fathers of Confederation.

But there is more than symbolism behind the name— the road literally links Canada's two Central provinces, and binds the English and the French nations to each other. And from a sheer numbers perspective, over half of Canadians live alongside the Quebec City–Windsor corridor that the 401 services.

But if the highway celebrates two pillars of Canada's founding, it also overlooks the uncomfortable truths at the core of the tale Canada tells itself. The national origin story is a lot more complicated than the marriage of the English and the French—Canada was also built through the systematic and intentional dispossession and neglect of the country's First Nations.

The 401 sails past the Tyendinaga First Nation, where the water is not safe to drink. The Mohawk territory has been under boil water advisory for a decade. *A decade*. Southern Ontario is an impossibly prosperous region, in part because of the 401. And yet cars pass by Tyendinaga, unaware of what its residents have to do just to simply drink a glass of water.

The highway can help tell your story, but it can also help you avert your gaze from what you don't want to see. The highway is, sometimes, a lie that we tell ourselves.

❧

Mama is soft-hearted. Baba is stubborn. That's the way it's always been.

So it was no surprise that my relationship with Mama snapped back right away, even though I didn't return to live at home. I rented a room at a friend's house, three blocks away from my parents. I wanted to be close, but not *too* close.

I dropped by often, and had meals with Mama. We went shopping. Sometimes I came over to drive her places. Within a few weeks, it was like the whole rift had never happened. She even began asking questions about Emily.

Baba was another matter. Faced with my stubbornness, he dug in his heels. It would be months before we had a conversation *at all*. When I visited, he had his back to me, typing just a *little* too loudly on his computer. By this point, he'd transitioned from running convenience stores to driving a taxi. And seeing his car on the road always made me want to hide. I was shattered by the fact we weren't talking.

Months later, when we did begin to talk, it was because of a fragile peace accord brokered by Mama. It had one rule of engagement—Baba and I could talk about anything in the world except for Emily.

That meant that I could once again share with Baba the triumphs and the joys and the struggles of my life, but with a strict boundary. If Mama asked me a question about my relationship, he would shut down and exit the conversation until such time that he could re-join it. I hated this arrangement but I agreed to it because it kept my dad in my life. It tethered me to him—this man I so admired.

We kept it up for years. We kept it up when Emily and I moved into our first apartment together, a strange little unit in a student housing tower just off campus. I continued to call and visit, and we talked about everything but the most important person in my life. I could tell him all about how we hosted extravagant potlucks in our tiny apartment, which never seemed to run out of space for friends. But I couldn't tell him who I hosted these potlucks with.

We never spoke about Emily even after I asked her to marry me in that apartment and she said yes. I wanted nothing more than Baba's big crushing hugs, the kind where he shakes the person he's hugging with the force of his excitement. But I couldn't even tell him about it.

We kept up this act as I pulled up in the packed U-Haul to say goodbye to Mama and Baba one last time before Emily and I moved to Toronto—two and a half hours westbound, down the same highway that had brought me here. I hugged them goodbye and got in the truck. I felt the weight of the miles between us.

᪥

Emily and I got married on the hottest day of the year in 2012. Mama was there, having long come around to meeting—then cherishing—Emily.

Five hours before the ceremony, I stood in the parking lot of the hotel and called Baba. I wanted to hear his voice on my wedding day, and I wanted to give him another chance to change his mind. "If you leave in an hour," I stuttered, "you can make it."

"Make it where?"

"To my wedding, Baba."

"Amin . . ."

"Baba, I wish you were here. Your seat is reserved for you if you'd like to use it."

"I'm sorry. But I can't come because I don't approve."

From the parking lot of the Waterfront Hotel Burlington, I could catch a glimpse of the highway. I could see the traffic humming. And I cried, realizing there was to be no last-minute miracle, no magical intervention that would bring Baba down the same road today.

I cried, watching for a car that would never come.

❧

Two years later, I was visiting friends in Kingston for the weekend, when Baba asked if I could spare a few minutes to meet him at a Wendy's just off the 401, on my way out of town.

I pulled in, not sure what to expect. I planned to adhere to the long-brokered agreement not to mention Emily. We sat down together. Baba let out a long sigh and took off his glasses, his signal that what he's about to say has been weighing heavily on him.

"I want to apologize. I have been unfair to you," he began. "And that poor girl . . ." He trailed off. "I have been cruel and unkind, and for that I am so sorry." I stayed silent. "I've been stubborn your whole life, and I know that. I thought this was the way to get through life. I had a hard time adjusting to you becoming your own person, and it made me miss out on the things that make you happy, and make your life beautiful."

As we went our separate ways, Baba said, "Tell Emily I want to meet her."

I took off down the highway, my heart a vast expanse, struck by the ways words can put you back together. I'd never known a lightness like this.

TWELVE

A River Runs Through It

"Do you know what your name means?"

I heard the voice before I saw the face as I slid into the back seat of an Uber outside the airport in Nashville. "I do," I replied, buckling my seat belt. It's a question I hear often from older Arab men who glimpse my name in the app. "It means 'honest and trustworthy'; it's what they often called Prophet Muhammad." A beat. "Mashallah," he replied. "Some people still remember."

I looked up and noticed that my driver looked a little like . . . everyone I grew up with. His moustache looked like my dad's older brother's; his gap-tooth smile looked like my old neighbour's; his grey, full head of hair reminded me of my math teacher in Khartoum.

I knew right away he was Sudanese. Within minutes, we were trading stories: he was rhyming off names of families he knew in my old neighbourhood, and I was offering stories from the last time I was in Sudan. It's a thing Sudanese people do: we sit and excavate our connections. We carefully untangle our roots, looking for the ways we might be tethered to one another.

He shared that he'd come to America after a brief stint in Saudi Arabia, then the U.K. I asked him what had brought him to Nashville—why *here*? "*Nas taybeen*," he offered. The root word for *taybeen* is *teeba*, which doesn't have a direct translation in English, but perhaps the closest approximation is a disposition toward tenderness and kindness. It's the kind of comment I was used to my parents making to each other after they met new people and were struck by their generosity.

As we pulled off the highway, he noticed my destination: the Country Music Hall of Fame and Museum. "What brings you to town?" he asked. I answered that I was a journalist who was here for work. What I should have said was: I am here following a faint thread I picked up a few years ago. A curiosity. An inkling. An emotional connection my body noticed before my brain did—which is that country music and folk music and other iterations of American roots music give me the same feeling that Sudanese music does.

I notice it in my shoulders first: they drop, sensing safety. I breathe a little easier. The tension I am holding in my body dissipates, and a smile steals its way onto my face. I get a peaceful, easy feeling, like there is no conflict I am meant to resolve. Country music holds a deep familiarity, well beyond the intellectual. Country songs about places I've never been to land on my ears and I am softer, like somehow this music is taking me home. I can't help but be flooded with this feeling, and I wanted to understand it. So: yeah, I was here for work.

At the end of the ride, I thanked my driver/friend/ excavation companion/now close relation because he knew a guy who once married my neighbour's cousin. He insisted, the way my people do, that I cancel my hotel reservations and come stay at his house. I insisted that I could never impose like that, as though I'd even entertain the thought. But the insistence is a sport to my people, and so we went at it. After the customary twenty-one rounds, he relented and wished me a good time.

❯

As far as museum buildings go, the Country Music Hall of Fame is not exactly subtle. Equidistant straight vertical windows cut through the stone front of the building, making the structure resemble the keys of a piano. The museum itself gently recedes, then at its deepest point it curves back out again—from the air, it looks like a giant bass clef. At one end, the distinct rotunda that houses the Hall of Fame portion of the museum takes the familiar shape of the grain silos you find all over the countryside, because what's the point of an understated metaphor? If you can read music, you'll see that the stone bars outside the rotunda have the notes for "Will the Circle Be Unbroken," which the Carter Family made famous. Inside the rotunda, it's less subtle: as you peruse the names of Hall of Famers, the words *will the circle be unbroken* hang directly over your head.

I wasn't sure what I was hoping to find by coming here. But as I made my way around the curated exhibits, I saw a white woman point at a sign that read: "Enslaved African musicians introduced the banjo to Americans." She said to her companion, "I didn't know this. It should be bigger." She wasn't wrong about this. It should be bigger. *Ah. This is why I came here.*

The popular narrative of country music tells a tidy story, which is that it's the domain of white people. For this reason, I'm never more Black than when I talk about my love for country. By which I mean: I'm never more aware of my Blackness than when I'm receiving quizzical looks in return. The unspoken onus in the moment is: *Explain yourself—how do* you *like country?*

The look is, in part, because too many people are

a little too sure they know country music. They don't even have to like it to think this. In fact, the folks who *don't* listen to country are very likely to claim knowledge of the subject matter: of country songs and what they're about; of the kind of people who listen to country—their values, their likes and dislikes.

This recurring narrative of country music is loathsome and a bit glib. It's tired on the best of days. But for someone like me, who has found that country music evokes home in ways most music doesn't, it's downright incoherent.

But there in the Hall of Fame—in small font, but still there—is the Big Truth of country. At its core, the music is a mystical marriage of the African banjo and the Western European fiddle.

The histories of the people who brought these instruments to America couldn't be more different. The enslaved clung to the banjo for hope in the face of brutality and death. The white fiddlers, on the other hand, had it easy. Yet these groups had in common the fact that they were homesick—longing for what they once knew. Their flavours of homesickness merged and thoroughly combined, and we got what eventually became country music.

It is, by default, a genre born of longing. It is music born of people looking for a new place to call home, while trying to remember where they came from. A glimmer that wouldn't die, or more accurately couldn't be killed. Country, then, is a music of rooting and orienting yourself—a genre as compass, a stretching backward to move forward.

It is this feeling that houses me when I lose myself in country: the chords ring out and paint a scene of remembrance, of connection to a past long gone. It's been two decades since I left Sudan, but the twang of the banjo projects outward and reminds me that the river that is my history passes through other lands.

❥

Growing up, my main sources of musical education were Baba and my uncle Foofoo. From Baba, I learned to revere the way Abdel Karim al-Kabli bends the strings of the oud. "Listen," he'd say with his eyes closed, as if to visualize the melodies. "This is real music." From Foofoo, I learned to listen for the emotionality in Mostafa Sid Ahmed's voice. Foofoo was political and passionate, and he liked his music the same way. Sid Ahmed could make you cry with the tremble in his delivery, the depth of the stories he told in song.

Giants like Sid Ahmed and al-Kabli built their reputations on elaborate poetry and complex melodies. They emphasized songwriting and storytelling, and paid tributes to the giants who came before them. The classic artists of the past sang songs that became a part of *Haqeeba Al-f'n*, or "the Briefcase of Art." The *Haqeeba* (Briefcase) is shorthand for the towering works of Sudanese music—a generation of singers and songwriters whose work is so treasured that it was deemed essential to protect and teach as canon.

The other major influence on the music I loved was my cousin Waleed. Gregarious and warm, with a smile that never leaves his face, for a stretch of time he was (and still occasionally is) a well-connected and sought-after backup singer. The best singers wanted to work with him. On the nights he had a gig, he brought me to parties with him, and set me up with a plate of food and a seat beside the stage. The deal was, if I was quiet and stayed out of trouble, I could come to more of these parties. And so I watched a new generation of singers burst onto the scene, entertaining people at weddings or birthday parties or playing one-off gigs. I'd watch the hottest new artists perform months before their debut albums would actually come out.

Waleed had an eye for the up-and-comers who were going to make it big. And there were two main ways for new singers to make it big: sing *Haqeeba* songs—songs that have already earned their place in people's hearts—or sing songs that shock people into noticing you. So, between Baba and Foofoo, who insisted that I learn the pillars of Sudanese song, and Waleed, who was enmeshed in the world of emerging artists, my childhood featured a well-rounded education.

The division within most Sudanese music is not pop vs. other genres, but rather by age and what each generation of artists sings about. The established singers might croon about the way a beloved's eyes look under the moonlight by the water. Young singers who want to stand out sing songs that scandalize the older generations and capture the energy of youth—perhaps by describing aggressive courtship.

But regardless of generation, a great deal of Sudanese music is built around description of place: the young artists sing about specific neighbourhoods to win favour with audiences; the established artists paint a picture of nature—the banks of the river, the breeze, the roses. The young and the old both sing of traditions; the elders revering them, the youngsters curious if they can bend them just a little.

And regardless of generation, they all sing of the Nile. The Nile is the heartbeat of Sudanese song.

When I came to Canada, the cassette tape in Baba's

car, a Dodge Caravan, was always occupied with a Kabli album. One mainstay of the car stereo was Kabli's *Amir Al Oud*, named after his frequent nickname, the Prince of the Oud.

It begins with a lengthy speech to one of the foundational *Haqeeba* poets and songwriters, Hassan Attia. "I felt an urgency," Kabli says, "that the younger generations must be made aware of your brilliance. It is our duty that this brilliance be passed on, and be known."

He delivers these lines before he launches into "Al Khortoum," a song with rich imagery about the flowers that grow on the banks of the Nile; about how Khartoum is the jewel of the country; about the way the Nile worships at the shores of the city, and how seeing it every day reminds us of who we are. It is a tribute to the river that runs through it.

✔

I was introduced to country music in a roundabout way. I was humming The Band at work when a colleague suggested that I give The Byrds a try, starting with their sixth album, *Sweetheart of the Rodeo*, and I agreed.

Sweetheart is an unusual place to delve into The Byrds. Up until that point in their career, they'd blended folk and rock and delved into psychedelia, but *Sweetheart* is a whole other terrain. It begins with "You Ain't Goin' Nowhere," a Bob Dylan cover that soars with twangy sliding guitars and smooth vocals. The album is a tight eleven-song record that is now recognized as the model for fusing country and rock and roll.

Though I'd never heard of The Byrds, the album was immediately familiar. Here I was, fifteen years removed from Sudan, and the music immediately reminded me of the music I grew up hearing. Musically, it sounded more sparse than the metal and pop I'd been listening to since arriving in Canada. The spaces between the notes gave me the same feeling Sudanese music gives me: they let you recede deeper into yourself, and your eyes soften and you become pensive, connected to something bigger. This was music that spent its time describing its natural surroundings with delicate care: "Hickory Wind" ("In South Carolina there are many tall pines / I remember the oak tree when we used to climb"), and "Blue Canadian Rockies," and "You Ain't Goin' Nowhere." It concerned itself with mining personal history ("I am a pilgrim and a stranger / Traveling through this wearisome land") and reflecting on God.

In this web of feelings, I recognized myself. The music connected with the archive of Sudanese music I carry inside of me, which shaped my aesthetic and emotional tastes. These were the subject matters that made up the vast majority of the music I listened to in Sudan. *Now that's what I call music*, so to speak. I thought— so you're telling me there's a whole genre of music that can speak to me like this?

Sweetheart almost never was. When The Byrds set out to make a record, their intention was to make a concept album: the plan was to distill the whole history of American popular music into a double album. Sure, some elements of country would be in it. But so would jazz and rhythm and blues and swing and every other genre, and it would span all the way to the birth of rock and roll. From there on, the album would try to predict the future by experimenting with electronic music. Frankly, it was the kind of concept album you'd come up with while a little high.

But there was an unexpected problem: The Byrds needed new members after David Crosby and Michael Clarke left, leaving just Roger McGuinn and Chris Hillman as official members of the band. They set about recruiting, and settled on a young kid, twenty-one-year-old Gram Parsons.

Parsons came on board with his own idea of what The Byrds should do—he wanted to capture the spirit of a "Cosmic American Music." His plan was to fuse a bunch of forms of roots music—mostly country, but with elements of folk and blues and soul. Eventually, the rest of The Byrds shelved their original concept and followed his lead.

Parsons felt that country music told the story of America better than any other genre. It was the river that ran through it.

∨

Sudanese music doesn't sound like anything other than itself. This is in part because, like the country, the music was born out of conflict. Just as Sudan's identity is a delicate dance between Arab influences and African traditions, the music contains the same careful mix.

Melodically, the instrumentation resembles what you'd find in an Arab pop orchestra. We borrowed staples of Egyptian music, with violins introducing the melody and countermelody and doing the lifting in replying to the singer. The oud fills in the liminal spaces, like an ornament atop the countermelody. The rest of the orchestration is filled out with accordions and saxophones. But the *rhythms* are distinctly African—and more precisely, sub-Saharan. I learned to drum a three-against-two pattern on the breakfast table, before I could even speak. When I'm stressed, I find myself subconsciously tapping a six-beat. These are rhythms that do not leave your body after they enter it.

As far as the singing goes, the delivery moves between the identities, too—there are the elaborate vocal runs that feel distinctly Arab, buttressed by the strings performing the melodies, living alongside the yelps of African musical traditions.

Other influences frequently find their way in. Funk guitar and reggae rhythms are not unusual in Sudanese music. But its nature remains singular. You could never mistake Sudanese music for the songs of another nation. There is nothing ubiquitous about it.

∨

From The Byrds, I found Emmylou Harris, and she sang with a sensitivity that reminded me of Hanan al-Nil, the legendary songbird who long ago renounced music and declared it forbidden. The specificity of John Prine's songs evoked what I knew of Mohammed Wardi's music: poets for the soul, wielding precision as the key to their art.

Even in the ascendant bro-country movement that was sweeping country music in the mid-2010s, I recognized the push-pull of respecting the genre's conventions while trying to figure out where to bend them—Florida Georgia Line and Jamal Farfoor may appear to have little in common, but their posture in their respective genres is the same.

Though I came to country music late, I found in it the same river that runs through Sudanese music: it's the same longing for home, the same probing for identity, the same searching to construct your story through music.

The Uber driver in Nashville noted that Southerners are *nas taybeen*, "generous people." But there is another translation of the root word *teeba*, and that's "type"— used to signify the essence of a person (e.g. *Teebtu kidda*, "That's just his nature."). He could've been saying: *These people are like us.*

Once, at a country music festival in the middle of nowhere, I felt a hand tap my shoulder. I turned around to find a young Black man, perhaps five or six years younger than me. He shook my hand and turned to his white friend and said, "I told you there'd be one," and then hurried away.

I wondered if he meant he knew there'd be at least one other person who'd picked up the map and found that surely country music was the way home.

THIRTEEN

The Estrangement

The day we left Sudan, Mama said I could have my pick of rides to the airport. The options were bountiful: there was a small armada of cars seeing us out, each loaded with family members and friends and neighbours who insisted on coming with us.

I chose to ride with my aunt, two cousins, and a neighbour, in the third car of this heartbreak motorcade. I sat in the back, behind the passenger seat, my eyes already raw from the tearful goodbyes we'd exchanged at home. I wore thick sunglasses and hung my head out of the window for the entirety of the ride, trying to inhale one last breath of Khartoum's hot July air, trying to memorize every detail so that I would never forget.

We drove past the burger place I loved—Estella put eggs on their burgers and proudly proclaimed that "the

French do it," and it was glorious every time. We drove past the doctor's office where my thumbs had been pricked a thousand times to do blood tests for malaria. We drove past the barber shop where the barber always greeted me with a hug and, after finishing the haircut—a 1 all the way around—would always say, "I'm not sure why you want to look like an egg, but here you go!"

We drove past Hajja Ghalia's tree. This big shady tree on the side of the road was a key waypoint for me on the walk to my uncle's house, and a familiar stop for most kids in the neighbourhood. Hajja Ghalia's stand was famous for being the best snack stop in the area. Every day, she sat under the same tree and prepared fresh cucumbers and nuts, tossed in a spicy chutney. On the extra-hot days, if you got there early enough, she had freezies, too. She knew all of our names and our parents' names, and treated us like her children. I kicked myself for not having returned to Hajja Ghalia's tree before leaving, and I wondered when I'd have her spicy cucumbers again.

And then we drove past the movie theatre. Cinema al-Halfaya was owned and operated by a family friend, and it was where I'd spent multiple nights a week for the last two or three years. I knew it well—its single screen was about six storeys high, and because it was an open-air theatre, screenings couldn't begin before dusk. I knew the perfect row to sit in if you wanted a good view *and* the ability to grab another pop while the projectionist changed reels.

The theatre rarely showed films in English, and never showed Arabic movies. The draw was Bollywood. Bollywood films got the crowd going—cheering for the good guys, or hollering at an elaborate action sequence. Bollywood films are also not short. On a double-feature night, I'd catch both the 8 p.m. screening and the 11:30 p.m. show. Mama granted me permission to stay up that late only for the cinema, and I made sure to exercise it.

It occurred to me as we drove past the theatre on our way to the airport that, for all the hours I logged in that movie theatre, I'd never asked: Why hasn't there been a Sudanese movie at this cinema the *whole* time I've been coming here? What would a Sudanese film even be *about*? Next, I wondered if Canada had Bollywood movies, too. (It does.)

I do not remember the last words I said to all of my cousins and all of my aunts and all of my uncles before Mama and I went past airport security. I do remember the look on their faces: it was a look that said *hold on to us*. It was a look that said *remember that this is precious*.

It was a look that said *don't drift, because this is home.* I assured the flotilla of family that I'd be back soon. That I'd come visit, and I'd visit often. You know, like a liar.

∨

Sometimes history weighs on you in ways you don't expect. After a screening of *You Will Die at Twenty* at the 2019 Toronto International Film Festival, I did not move from my chair for what felt like an eternity. Moviegoers shuffled out of their seats in preparation to get to their next film, and staff began ushering people out to get the theatre ready for the next show, but I was not ready to move.

Twenty is a drama set in a small village near the Nile, and it tells the story of Muzamil, a young boy who, shortly after his birth, a Sufi mystic says will die when he reaches the age of twenty. The film is an adaptation of Hammour Ziada's short story "Sleeping at the Foot of the Mountain." It is an extraordinary piece of cinema. It was also only the second Sudanese feature film I'd ever seen.

Twenty had buzz coming into TIFF. At the Venice International Film Festival, its Sudanese director Amjad Abu Alala won the "Lion of the Future" award for best first feature. It also helped that its mythology was built before anyone had seen a single frame: the movie was completed during the unrest of a budding anti-government revolution in Sudan—the same government that had cracked down on cinema thirty years earlier and suppressed Sudan's film industry. That the film was completed at all was an unlikely achievement. *Twenty* is said to be only the eighth or ninth feature film completed since Sudan's independence in 1956.

When *Twenty* found me, I was nearly a decade into a career that includes, among other things, film criticism and culture writing. I know the language of film—I spent a great deal of my teens and even more of my twenties in love with the big screen. I know what to look for, and *Twenty* checked all the boxes of a major film accomplishment. And yet it was not Sébastien Goepfert's stunning cinematography or Abu Alala's familiar fable-narrative that took my breath away.

Instead, it was the film's world-exploding intimacy. I was moved by *Twenty*'s careful treatment of the customs and dialects and superstitions that I grew up knowing in my bones. At the core of *Twenty* is a battle of modernity against tradition—the desire to keep up with the West, set against the tether to traditions. Every family I knew went through an iteration of this battle. *Twenty* is a film rooted in a Sudan I immediately recognized, and I felt bowled over by that recognition. Every shot filled me with the urge to shout *these are people I know.*

Toward the climax of *Twenty*, we see Muzamil's mom, Sakina, attend a Zar ceremony. Zar rituals were long associated with exorcism of demons, and believed to be carried out to banish evil spirits. I grew up with Zar as something spoken of in whispers and hushed tones. I heard adults talk in quiet voices about those who went to Zars as either quacks or people too comfortable taking on demons. I heard rumours that Zar involved sacrificing chickens (or was it goats? bunnies?) and doing immoral things (like *what*, I was never told). I knew that the repressive government did not approve of Zars, and that made them even more dangerous.

Two streets over from our home in Khartoum, there was a house known to host Zar rituals. In daylight, we crossed the street when we walked past it. At night, we avoided the street altogether. On the nights they hosted a Zar, the whole neighbourhood heard the drums and the singing and the wailing well into the night. The mystery of *what the hell does a Zar look like?* intensified in my mind with every beat of the drum.

In *Twenty*, Sakina goes to the Zar in search of answers. It was the first time I'd seen a Zar. It's a claustrophobic scene, shot with handheld cameras coming in close on every dance move and every bead of sweat. Watching it, I felt the thrill of a great mystery finally being resolved. *So this is what a Zar looks like.* During a post-screening Q&A, Abu Alala told the audience that the scene was an authentic Zar, not a recreation: he'd asked the women of the village where he shot *Twenty* to host a ritual, and he'd instructed his entire crew to hang back. Only Abu Alala and his cinematographer were allowed in, and they took great care not to say a single word, just capture what they were seeing.

Twenty elegantly distilled conflicts I knew and answered questions I had. It gave a convincing resolution to what a Sudanese movie might be about: the ways we are at war with ourselves; the ways we protest our history while also fighting to hold on to it. *Remember that this is precious.*

∨

The first thing I noticed was the sting of watching the intimacy between my cousins that I'd missed out on. They'd been without me for nearly a decade. They'd developed handshakes and hungers, secrets and stories, without me. Their eyes could speak in a code that I was not privy to.

I arrived in Khartoum in the summer of 2009, my first and only trip back since I left in 2000. Baba and I were greeted by a small army of uncles and cousins. We landed in the late afternoon, and on the car ride to the place we were to stay, I grew silent as I took in the city. It still sounded like a cacophony of horns and tire screeches. The roundabouts were still chaotic as all hell. But there was also a distinctly different flavour: the cars that drove beside us blasted Lil Wayne and Kanye West alongside Ahmed Alsadig and Jamal Farfoor. Some blocks had been rebuilt in a mode I hadn't seen in Khartoum before: the strip mall.

On that ride, for the first time it occurred to me that the word we use for expats is *mughtarbeen*, singular *mughtarib*, which could have multiple root words: there's *Gharb*, or "West"—so *mughtarbeen* could mean "those who are in the West"; *or* there's *ghareeb*, meaning "stranger." *Mughtarbeen*, "the estranged ones." I've frequently heard Mama say "*al-ghurba ha'ra.*" The estrangement burns.

And burn it did. My return to Sudan was for a cousin's wedding, and weddings in Sudan last a lifetime. That meant I could see all of my family all the time, but seeing them stung because it was a constant reminder of the ways we no longer understood one another. And we are talking about little things here—it's always the little things—but everyone noticed. How I wanted to disappear after I stumbled when asked to do the call to prayer; how I got flustered when I didn't know my way around the house I grew up in. *The estrangement burns*. Each time, they exchanged a look and helped me find my way, but I still felt like a burden. Like I was standing just outside.

Since 2009, that feeling has never abated. It's the feeling that sets in when I read Sudan's news, which I still occasionally do, or make an effort to listen to new Sudanese songs, which I am adamant about. It's a feeling that my right to know and enjoy those things is up for debate.

I was twenty-one the last time I was in Sudan, and I sensed that I was changing, and that Sudan was changing, but we weren't changing together. I sensed that I was working to change my idea of Sudan, but Sudan was relatively unconcerned. *You left, so we'll go on without you*, it seemed to be saying to me.

If that sense of estrangement is a low hum at all times, it has occasional spikes. Some are benign, like when I'm faced by a line in a song I don't understand. Others are sharper, like when I meet new Sudanese people and I feel myself trying to impress them with how much I still remember about Sudan. I end up feeling like my efforts come off as desperate.

What connects these moments of being thrust into the estrangement is the feeling of being on trial. *You are not Sudanese enough*, I imagine my fictional accusers charging me. *You've forgotten how we live.*

But the estrangement was never as acute as when watching the ousting of Omar al-Bashir. Sudan was in the throes of a historic revolution, one that would see the toppling of a dictator who had been in power since I was a year old—and all I could do was *tweet*? Every day I watched cousins be in the thick of it: the standoffs against corrupt security forces; the sit-ins where people did their best to protect one another. I knew that if I was there—if I had never left—I would be with them. I would trade blows with security forces, or throw rocks. Something. *Anything.* But as a brutalizing paramilitary group carried out an attack on protesters, all I could do was . . . write op-eds. The cousins I grew up with were together, handing out food and water for those who needed it.

During the revolution, Mama didn't sleep. All she did was call people or leave them voice notes. For days on end, she gave me updates—only they weren't news stories, they were the names of specific people we knew, and what they were up to.

Even now, in a time of non-revolution, Mama's phone doesn't stop ringing. The pings are constantly going off. That's the thing about becoming a stranger: you decide how involved you want to be. No one is going to invite you. And sometimes it's a little too easy to let yourself drift away.

❧

I left the screening of *Twenty* and immediately called Mama. I asked her to clear her schedule because she *needed* to see this Sudanese movie at the festival. As it turned out, she was way ahead of me: the Sudanese community in Hamilton, where she lives, was already buzzing about *Twenty* and were organizing a few cars that would make the trek. Mama said she wasn't sure if she could track down a ticket, and I told her I'd sort out that part.

The second screening of *Twenty* was markedly different from the first: this one was filled almost completely with Sudanese people. By this point, the revolution in Sudan had reached the stage of arguing over what kind of government would replace Bashir, with most people calling for the end of military rule. Abu Alala's speech introducing the film was interrupted by the common slogan shouted in the streets of Khartoum (*Hurreeya!*

Madaneeya! Civil rights!) and the atmosphere felt like a festive reunion. The audience sang songs I knew, and I quietly joined in with the parts I remembered.

As the lights dimmed, I stopped watching the movie and started watching how the bodies responded to what was onscreen. I watched for the claps, for the laughs, for the smiles. I watched for the same relief I'd felt seeing *Twenty* the first time. And watching everyone in the audience delight and weep and be moved by a story so familiar made me realize that in the estrangement, you become a stranger to yourself, too.

I suddenly wished I could see Mama—see everyone in that theatre—walking along the rose bushes on the banks of the Nile, in the streets of Khartoum, in a space they called home. I pictured this parallel image of Mama, the one I'd never seen but wished I had: she's young, she goes to film festivals, she moves in spaces she knows to be her own. I pictured them all young, taking to the streets of Khartoum and demanding a civil government.

This was not how I knew her. This was not how I knew any of the people who saw *Twenty* that day. I mostly knew them as mamas and babas and aunties and uncles who went to work, and tended to the Sudanese part of the hyphen like it was a small garden;

it was work to make something grow there—and work they happily did, but it was still a lot of labour.

∨

I have a recurring dream that is a fictional continuation of a memory. The memory is from the last time I was in Sudan, in 2009: Baba and my uncle and I went to visit the farm I grew up visiting my whole childhood. The farmhouse was intact, the tomatoes were flourishing, the high ground that abruptly dropped as if it were bowing before the shores of the Nile still looked the same. In the memory, my uncle asks if the farm is still as I remember it, and I sheepishly nod and go quiet. In the dream, I say nothing, but my knees give out and I crumble to the ground weeping.

The memory is incomplete without the dream: the dream stitches together my adult self with the child that left Sudan. In the dream, I am weeping and asking for forgiveness. Forgiveness for leaving all of this. Forgiveness for missing birthdays and weddings and heartbreaks and revolutions. Forgiveness for not realizing long ago that all of this is worth crying over.

FOURTEEN

Roads (Part V)

It's amazing how in one highway bus ride, you can become a first-year oncology student.

An hour earlier, a kind doctor with a gentle tone delivered the news to me and Mama: the biopsy results came back, and "it's a tiny spot of cancer, smaller than a pea. We'll operate and get that thing out, okay?" My eyes found Mama's eyes, took in how her gaze shifted to somewhere beyond the doctor, because all she heard was "cancer."

I listened intently, taking notes. Stage 1 cancer, still very small and not particularly aggressive; it would be best to just remove the cancer with a quick surgery and follow it up with a round of chemotherapy.

Cancer has been the spectre that haunts Mama's side of the family. Her parents; one of her older brothers; the aunts she loved most. All gone because of cancer. So she didn't hear the specifics of her case; she just saw herself in everyone who died before her. Just a year ago, a cousin she considered a sister had died in her arms after a vicious fight with cancer—a fight during which Mama made it her business to nurse this cousin back to health. I could tell that all of these ghosts were flooding her field of vision.

We thanked the doctor, and when he left the room, Mama collapsed with her head in my hands. We hugged and cried together.

I picked a dark corner for the bus ride home, so I could weep in peace. But I could only muster up a few minutes of crying. Instead, I found myself downloading podcasts and reading public medical journals on breast cancer, arming myself for Mama's coming fight. By the time I returned to Toronto, I could give a short lecture on breast cancer. The highway won't let you give up.

v

I recently got in touch with my eighth-grade teacher to ask about her memories of my time in her class. Seared into her brain, she said, was the first parent-teacher conference. She told my parents about my areas of struggle, and where I needed to do a lot of work. She said she'd never forget how Baba turned to me and with perfect seriousness said, "If these grades don't improve, I am sending you back to Sudan."

It's a familiar threat to first- and second-generation immigrants. For years, if I overstepped boundaries I'd hear it. I never understood it to be a real possibility— more of a brandishing of the biggest tool they had in their arsenal if I didn't listen: their disappointment. If I drove them to the point of wanting to send me "back to Sudan," they were saying that uprooting their whole lives for a better life for us here had failed. This weaponized guilt always had the last word.

I began to see them as Immigrant Parents. As their preoccupation became the management of my identity, I began to reduce theirs. Slowly, I took the colours out of my image of Mama and Baba—the warm, tender, funny parents. They became the sum of the limitations they put on me.

But this was never the full picture. The Immigrant Parent idea is built in the same way, regardless of race— so there must be something bigger going on. And what I couldn't see then were the forces that might make Mama and Baba transform into more intensely adopting this Immigrant Parent identity.

I heard them repeating stories to each other of other children of Sudanese families. There was Hatim, who, *astagfirullah*, got his grade 11 girlfriend pregnant. Now, his family had sent all his siblings back to Sudan for an extended visit, to remind them of what Sudanese people were about. Then there was Nasir, who got in with the wrong crowd and was going to serve two years in prison. These stories, I realized later, weren't whispered in our home as gossip. These were my parents' worst fears, and every time they heard a new story, they tightened the leash.

Mama got double takes all the time because she covered her hair. At their most innocent, they were looks of curiosity, at their worst they were racist glances. But if you're met with enough of those looks in one day, you start to walk differently. She was aware of the everyday racism that confronted her, and she worried that it confronted me, too. So she was protective—denying any request I made to leave the house.

Perhaps the most pressing force that weighed down on them, and accelerated their transformation to Immigrant Parents in my eyes, was capitalism. Mama and Baba both came from prominent families in Sudan. Baba's great-grandfather was a significant sheikh, a learned Muslim scholar. There is a village just outside

Khartoum and a neighbourhood in the city named after him. When we walked through the neighbourhood, everyone knew who we were. There are still people who sleep and pray next to my great-grandfather's tomb. They ask for guidance, and they spend weeks inside of it. On Mama's side, her great-grandfather was a Supreme Court judge. On the other side of Khartoum, there's a neighbourhood named after him, too.

But in Canada, things changed. They were at the mercy of capitalism, like everyone else. Often, when immigrants arrive, they don't have much with them— and for Baba, that was no exception. He pulled long days at the store; a thirteen- or fourteen-hour day was normal. Meanwhile, Mama pushed through an English as a Second Language course, and then a college cooking program so she could get a job as a line cook at a Greek restaurant—at forty-two, her first job since she was twenty-six.

My parents made this work, but it wore on them. With the little time they had left to parent, they were too exhausted to look closely while I dove into what Canada had to offer. So they tried to cut it off at the source by imposing curfews.

Immigrant Parents aren't born that way. They're created by the battle they wage against the forces lined

up at their door, threatening to take what they hold
dearest.

∨

On my drives to visit my parents, the highway became
the place I processed emotions. It's on that pavement
that the regrets poured in. I regretted not being more
gentle in disagreement. The shouting and the clashing.
I regretted the superiority I felt entitled to, and fully
inhabited, when I said I wanted to break free, not knowing that to them it read as *I want to break free from
everything that you are.* I regretted the unthinking cru-
elty, the time I spent waging war instead of cultivating
diplomacy or laying down a soil of tenderness. I regretted every moment I'd let them think that what I wanted
was distance from *them.* I regretted not recognizing
sooner that they were doing the best they could with
the tools they had.

Each trip made me softer. Love is a practice, a trail
you carve out by travelling the same path over and over
and over until it becomes familiar, until it lights the
way home.

History weighs on us most when we are its sole
custodians—when we are the ones who have to tell it to
the next generation. This is often forced, not chosen.

By coming to Canada, Mama and Baba no longer had a whole village of people that remembered their twists and turns, the peculiarities of their biography. They had me. One thorny and stubborn branch, while the rest of the tree grew elsewhere. I grew up in an ocean of their stories, with every family member a wellspring watering me. But now I was the sole headwater, passing on their complexities. This can feel heavy.

Out of the blue, Baba's hugs have been getting longer. His arms wrap all the way around, and hold on tightly. On Facebook and in text messages, he tells me he's proud of me; he is exuberant with heart emojis. But in person, he channels all of those emotions into one tight hug.

Out of the blue, my mother started saying "I love you." This was new for us: it has never been a part of my parents' literacy of love. Thirty-two years on this earth, and I'd never heard her say it. Now, after we say our goodbyes in Arabic, she shoehorns it in, in English.

She says the phrase in singsong, and I recognize this for what it is: an acknowledgement that this is a part of how I express love in a context that isn't in Sudan. It's an effort to speak to me across the divide between the worlds we inhabit.

But, like the highway, her arms are stretched out wide and she is reaching, reaching, because it's in the reaching that we find grace.

Elsewhere

There is no greater symphony of accommodation than a mosque in the West right after Eid prayers. It is a collection of greetings making room for one another. The custom is to greet strangers and friends alike, and celebrate a holy day. But in each mosque, these greetings are carried out in different ways.

There are cultures (Pakistan, Bangladesh) that do the triple hug (right, left, then right again). Other cultures (Syria, Iraq) that do a handshake and a double-cheek kiss—not to be confused with the cultures (Egypt) that *don't* do a handshake but do a triple-cheek kiss (right, left, then right again). Some (Sudan) do a left-shoulder touch, then a handshake, while others suffice with a hand to the heart.

The brave try to guess which kind of greeting is coming to them and wholeheartedly meet the greeting person there. The bold say *you know what, this is how we do it in my culture*, and take the lead. The meek—and I am proudly among them—stand still and let the hugs and kisses and shoulder touches land where they may.

On Eid morning, it's easy to imagine another context—each greeting in its own birthplace. There, everyone does the triple hug or the handshake/double-cheek kiss combo, and not just on Eid but for the many little celebrations of life. Perhaps an engagement gathering or a graduation party.

It's easy, too, to imagine how the performer of each greeting would have suspended using it in the everyday. Perhaps they stopped all at once, opting instead for the Western handshake or a hug. Perhaps they gave it up slowly: maybe they did it back when they arrived at the airport, but gradually it faded from regular life.

But on Eid morning, without fail, the mosque is filled with people who cart out their traditional hugs-and-kisses rituals, insisting on giving them air. On their faces, you see relief and remembrance. A look that says *this is how I say hello.*

❥

From time to time, I want to correct names that are not mine to correct. I will hear a person introduce themselves with a name that is a word I know to be Arabic, but is being pronounced incorrectly. In these moments, it is all I can do not to blurt out a clarification.

What I want to say is: *Look, the way it's been anglicized for you is wrong.* Or: *Look, you say "ha" but your name contains a ح, a letter that requires more from you. It requires that you force air from your throat, then stop it midway through your windpipe—here, let me teach you.*

Instead, I say, "Nice to meet you." Instead, I say, "What a beautiful name, is that Arabic?" But when I do this, what I am trying to say is: *In the very way you introduce yourself, there is a conflict. There is a distance between the real word and how you say it.*

I stop myself because I know this distance is treacherous terrain. I wonder if they know the word but they say it differently (wrongly!) so as to avoid having to deliver a phonetics lesson when they just want a coffee. Or perhaps it was their parents who passed on this pronunciation, having given up the attempts to teach the proper ح in between managing night shifts and language classes. Or what if the speaker has gone by an entirely different name (say, Stan) and this mangled word is a bridge back to a name they'd like to reclaim?

Whatever the reason may be, their name is not mine to correct. You don't go into people's homes and tell them their framed photos are hanging crooked. It's better to admire what they've chosen to put up.

∨

My daughter is four. On occasion, out of the blue, her eyes will light up as she asks: "Baba, tell me about Sudan." I tell her about the dusty unfinished roads I grew up on, and the bus I took to school. I tell her about my cousins, all one million of them. I tell her that they all know her name, they all ask about her all the time. On my phone, I scroll through pictures of family members and tell her a story about each one.

As we do this, she listens intently. She asks questions, like: "Don't they miss you?" ("Yes, they do, and I miss them all so much"); "When you moved to Canada, did they cry?" ("They did, and I did too"). When I finish, she has one last question: "Why do they know who I am? We've never met!" At the risk of over-ascribing intention to a four-year-old's questions, her aim seems clear: she is trying to figure out just how much room in her life she has to make for the part of her history that's from another place. It's the birth of her very own Elsewhere— a nebula of negotiation gathering a gravitational pull.

v

Elsewhere is a volcano, but it is one you walk into willingly. Elsewhere is a choice, and can only be a choice—you must care enough to bear the weight of the heaviness to which your heart is tethered. This is to say, you have agency in shifting your gaze from a once-home to a now-home. Elsewhere is for the middle children of diaspora, those who have definitely left but haven't exactly arrived.

You have to let yourself be reminded that a part of you is rooted in another place; face what is missing, the empty crevices that once contained what you now lack—an old way of greeting, a pronunciation of your name that is at best an approximation of the real thing—and say *thank you*, for it is because of this deficit that you know yourself. Elsewhere is a conscious choice to remain in the incomplete. Your Elsewhere is like no one else's, but it's the same in its fragile liminality. We live on a suspension bridge, and some days are windier than others.

Acknowledgements

You hold this book in your hands because a community of people have surrounded it with fierce protection and held it in deep tenderness, tenderness which I can never repay. You should know who they are:

Jared Bland, I'm humbled by your generosity and patience. Not (just) the patience of waiting past deadlines, but the greater patience: the willingness to wait until the softness comes, and the certainty that it will. Thank you for knowing when to push. Thank you for the compassion and rigour of your eye. Thank you for knowing there was a book somewhere here. I'm so grateful for the privilege of your friendship.

Sara Weiss, thank you for being interested from the start. For your care and clarity. For believing the very

Canadianness of this book is a strength, and letting it breathe. For the warmth and heart of your edits.

Martha Webb, for understanding the book before I did, and for helping me find the best version of what it could be. For knowing who needed the book before I did. Thank you for your guidance and counsel. I'm so fortunate to have a champion like you.

Gemma Wain, your close reading is a gift and an act of profound generosity. Thank you.

The team at McClelland & Stewart and Penguin Random House Canada: without you, this would be a word doc with a dream. Thank you for ferrying this book across rivers I will never understand. Thank you to Kimberlee Kemp, Scott Sellers, Sarah Howland, Erin Kelly, Tonia Addison, and Debbie Innes. Jennifer Griffiths, this cover is Elsewhere, manifest. Thank you Kristin Cochrane for the ways you've advocated for this book.

I hold so much gratitude for the thoughtful guidance of those who read early versions of these essays and pushed me to find something deeper and more true. Naheed Mustafa for reminding me to quit interrupting myself. Vicky Mochama for reminding me to find an enemy. Ishani Nath for always having the right reaction. Scaachi Koul, for having the widest range of expressing support. John Michael McGrath, for both your rambunctiousness and your reading. Thank you to Michael Naugler, Ally Garber, Shireen Ahmed for the ways you've enriched this book and my life.

Thank you to the friends who lifted me up as I wilted in the face of this enormity. I am so thankful to be tethered to you for support: Nick Day, for asking the right questions, always; Kerry Paterson, for never letting distance get in the way of a pep talk; Alina Kulesh, for being the sturdy tree in my life. Eric Bombicino and Harrison Lowman, for the toasts and the talks and the walks and the careful ways we have fastened our lives together.

Rory and Justice and Ellis, for lending your hearts and your literal actual home to bring this thing to life. Some of my proudest moments as a writer happened in your house. Thank you for always being close.

Rob and Amanda, your love touches every corner of my life. Thank you for remembering who I am on days when I can't quite do the same. Thank you for the vulnerable, unrestrained expressions of kindness and love.

Phil and Lori Burns, thank you for shouldering our family through this book, for the stolen weekends of writing, for making Amna feel safe and loved, for your unabating and unequivocal support, for always finding a new way to be there.

I am a lucky man in myriad ways but I am most blessed to be the son of Seif-Eldin Elamin Abdelmahmoud and Radia Ahmed Mohammed Abuelgasim Hashim. Please know your stories and your sacrifices and your successes colour every step of my walk. I am sorry for how long it took me to recognize your ways of expressing love, and I will spend the rest of my life making sure you know I love you.

Sudan, *ya baladi ya haboab*, this book is a flare in the sky, a signal, an attempt at reestablishing contact. I carry all the names with me, so I am always returning home.

Amna Eliot Abdelmahmoud, my heart, you are a growing branch as I write these words. One day, I hope you'll let them be a part of your map back to your roots. Thank you for teaching me resilience, thank you for the way you hold my face. Thank you for calling me Baba.

Emily Burns, my rock, my mountain. You are the only home I've ever needed. Thank you for reading this book more times than I have. Thank you for being the first reader and last reader always. Thank you for knowing where I keep my softness, and for reminding me to go get it. Thank you for making me feel shielded by the arms of love. When I put down this pen, let's go somewhere only we know.

ABOUT THE AUTHOR

ELAMIN ABDELMAHMOUD is a culture writer for *BuzzFeed News* and host of CBC's pop culture show *Pop Chat*. He was a founding co-host of the CBS Politics podcast *Party Lines,* and he is a contributor to The National's At Issue panel. His work has appeared in *Rolling Stone, The Globe and Mail,* and other outlets. When he gets a chance, he writes bad tweets.